THE RECOVERY
OF THE SACRED

The Recovery of
the Sacred

JAMES HITCHCOCK

A Crossroad Book
THE SEABURY PRESS · NEW YORK

The Seabury Press
815 Second Avenue
New York, N.Y. 10017

Library of Congress Cataloging in Publication Data

Hitchcock, James.
  The recovery of the sacred.

  "A Crossroad book."
  1. Liturgics.   2. Rites and ceremonies.   3. Holy,
The.   I. Title.
BV176.H57   264   73–17899
ISBN 0–8164–1150–6

FOR MY PARENTS

Contents

Preface

To write about the recovery of the sacred first of all implies that the phenomenon has been lost, which some persons in the contemporary Church may be inclined to deny. It is the book's thesis, however, that a qualitative change of the most profound significance has occurred since the Second Vatican Council and that this change is perceived by virtually everyone, even if the terminology used to describe it is not uniform.

One of the unhealthy aspects of contemporary religious life is the confusion and, ultimately, mistrust which is introduced by the equivocal use of terms. Thus innovating religious commentators may employ the traditional vocabulary, but it is often evident that they have altered the meanings of the words without acknowledgment. The concept of the sacred is one of the most important of these, since in traditional Catholic theology it has been generally employed to designate special persons, times, places, or objects viewed as having an especially holy character. To use it now to indicate qualities that are suffused through all of existence, or to designate merely what is most precious in the eyes of each individual, is to depart radically from this tradition. At a minimum those who would promote such departures and such redefinitions have an obligation to make clear what they are doing, to offer fair warning of the fullest implications of their work. It is the failure to do this, in matters of liturgy as in many other things, which as much as anything else has contributed to the tensions, uncertainties, and suspicions which now wrack the Church.

Understood in the traditional sense, the recovery of the sacred is thus something which some people will in principle oppose, since it has been the aim of a good deal of liturgical innovation precisely to exorcise the feeling for sacredness which permeated the Catholic Church before the present era of reform. This matter in the nature of things cannot be compromised. If one assumes that the worship of the Church is truly worship and that it has a sacral character, certain corollaries follow inevitably, which this book seeks to delineate. If, on the other hand, liturgy is perceived as having an essentially humanistic and worldly focus, then it will be necessary for those who believe this to oppose all efforts to resacralize it.

One of the book's major contentions is that a choice between these two attitudes is necessary and that a principal cause of the confusion and malaise which has affected the Church for nearly the past decade is the failure to recognize the implications of certain decisions, the tendency to muddle through haphazardly and without forethought.

It is also the book's purpose to argue that the tendency toward a desacralized liturgy, already partly achieved and destined to accelerate unless deliberate steps are taken to counteract it, cannot help but have the most profound effects on the whole life of the Church. These effects have already been felt in countless ways, primarily in the loss of coherent vision and purpose which followed the manipulation of the Church's most sacred symbols. Often liturgical change has been treated in quasi-isolation from the rest of life. It is now clear that one's basic approach to liturgy is likely to be both a reflection of and a catalyst to a whole range of values and beliefs. It is impossible to change basic symbols and rituals without changing also the life of the society whose symbols and rituals they are. This fact has not been sufficiently appreciated, although evidence of it now accumulates to an overwhelming degree.

Those persons who reject the concept of sacral worship as here set forth are for the most part individuals of sincerity, sensitivity, and good will. It is not particularly satisfying to argue against the validity of experiments which have usually been conceived and carried out with good intentions. This is particularly true when the experiments have been judged "successful" by all concerned. It is difficult to construct a truly modern yet effective liturgy, but it can be done.

At the same time the "success" of a liturgy cannot be judged simply on the basis of the subjective reactions of the participants. Liturgies can be rendered "effective" in a variety of ways which do violence to the fundamental meanings that Catholic liturgy is supposed to convey. It is partly by a failure to attend to meanings as well as to forms that the present condition of liturgical confusion has been allowed to develop.

The author is by profession a historian, not a liturgist or an anthropologist. Much of the thought contained here was originally stimulated by a historical investigation into the folk religion of Elizabethan England. A large debt will also be obvious to what is perhaps the most important religious book of the past decade, Mary Douglas's *Natural Symbols*. Had that work appeared before 1965, recent liturgical history might have been happier.

The author's claim to authority in liturgical matters is based primarily on a long interest in the subject as a "participant-observer," along with hard thought stimulated by that best of all goads to reflection—a painful experience which cries out to be made sense of. For a variety of reasons, many persons in the postconciliar Church have found the experience of liturgy painful; diagnosis does seem to ease pain, even when it does not take it away. The problems discussed here are primarily Roman Catholic liturgical problems, but they have relevance to a good deal of Episcopalian worship as well. The author has had some experience of Episcopal liturgy and of the questions raised by the introduction of the *Services for Trial Use.*

Finally, it is not possible to understand liturgy adequately on the theoretical plane without some powerful experience of living liturgy, which can persist as a glimpse of authenticity even amid a sea of poorer goods. It is probable that only an experience of powerful liturgy, prior to systematic reflection, is adequate to sustain genuine interest and understanding. For nearly twenty years the author has been indebted for that experience to Msgr. Martin B. Hellriegel, pastor of the Church of the Holy Cross in St. Louis.

JAMES HITCHCOCK

St. Louis
September 26, 1973
Feast of the North American Jesuit Martyrs

THE RECOVERY
OF THE SACRED

CHAPTER I

The Liturgical Revolution

In liturgy, as in most things, the year 1966 marked a crucial change in attitude on the part of many in the reform movement within the Roman Catholic Church. They had won what appeared to be a nearly complete victory over their opponents in the great arena of the Second Vatican Council. Liturgical reform was now mandated by the highest Church authorities and was being speedily, if not always enthusiastically, implemented in the parishes. The liturgists, after many decades when they had been contemptuously tolerated as harmless cranks or held in suspicion as probable heretics, had gained everything they had fought for, and more besides. They were to have not merely a partially vernacular Mass as a permissible option but a wholly vernacular Mass imposed practically as an obligation. In most churches the altars were turned to permit the celebrant to face the congregation during Mass. The weight of clerical authority was placed behind ceaseless exhortations to the people to pray together, sing together, "participate." Extra-liturgical devotions were in effect suppressed in many parishes. Bolder liturgists, having heard amid all the reverberating words of the Council only a single one—"change"—set to work devising new liturgies

3

which had greater or less degrees of connection with the old. But having tasted the fruits of victory after a war which had been long and often cold and lonely, they discovered that these were at best only mildly sweet, in fact nearly tasteless.

During its classic phase, which stretched from the great German and French Benedictine liturgical pioneers of the nineteenth century to the conclusion of the Second Vatican Council in 1965, the Liturgical Movement tried scrupulously to maintain a delicate balance of disparate (but not necessarily conflicting) elements: simplification but not at the expense of drama and ritual, closeness to the people but not so as to obscure mystery, reform but not to the extent of losing touch with tradition, correction of distorted popular beliefs but only to bring them into harmony with genuine orthodoxy.

A powerful and influential statement was the exposition of *The Mystery of Christian Worship* by the German monk Odo Casel, who argued that superficial liturgical changes would be ineffective without a profound reawakening within the Church of a sense of divine mystery—that in worship the believer is joined to Christ in sacramental union, an occurrence inexplicable in human terms and only dimly glimpsed by the subtlest theologians.

Dom Casel was sometimes criticized for his romanticism, and more cautious liturgists tempered his ideas with the Jesuit Josef Jungmann's *Mass of the Roman Rite*, a monument of scholarship which more than any other work both previewed the liturgical changes which the Council would decree and helped to bring them about. Jungmann demonstrated painstakingly the numerous accretions which had built up in the liturgy over the centuries and, more important, the numerous misunderstandings which had attached themselves to various parts of public worship, to the point where the original meanings were all but lost. Overall, however, Jungmann's purpose was to suggest paths of reform which might restore the worshipers' sense of the Mass as sacrifice, as the offering of Christ by the whole Church.

In the Church of England the Benedictine Gregory Dix traced *The Shape of the Liturgy* to its historic roots, analyzing with care and balance the tension between ritualism and puritanism in the Church, struggling like Jungmann to lay bare the essential core of the mystery—the oblation of Christ and union with Him by worshipers in deep faith.

As the Second Vatican Council was beginning, the French theologian Louis Bouyer was analyzing *Rite and Man: Natural Sacredness and Christian Liturgy*, arguing that both an unrestrained embrace of the ethos of the sacred—rites, mysteries, sacraments—and a severe puritanism are heretical from the standpoint of the Catholic tradition, pointing out the opposed dangers of regarding the words of worship as meaningless in themselves and hence as magic or merely as means for conveying doctrinal teaching. Christian ritual is saved from magic and from paganism by the persistent awareness that in the act of worship Christ is come among His people and the ritual is in fact the act of God.

In America the German refugee priest H. A. Reinhold, discussing *The American Parish and the Roman Liturgy*, attempted to apply the central insights of the Continental liturgists to the United States. He pointed out the degree to which the Latin language was a major barrier to comprehension and hoped for the adoption of the vernacular. At the same time he celebrated the stately austerity of the traditional liturgy and urged that the major liturgical task was to awaken the worshipers' sensitivity to sacred symbols, which in turn would give them access to the heavenly mysteries. On the eve of the Council he talked about *Bringing the Mass to the People* and wrote with optimism and assurance that this could be done without great difficulty, provided the basic spirit of the Roman liturgy—magnanimity, sobriety, solemnity, warmth—was retained.

The Vatican Council's *Constitution on the Sacred Liturgy* (*Sacrosanctum Concilium*) was a document infused with the classic spirit of the Liturgical Movement. Like nearly all the Council's decrees, it took pains to preserve the essential traditions even while allowing for change.

Among its pronouncements were:

For it is through the liturgy, especially the divine Eucharistic Sacrifice, that "the work of our redemption is exercised." The liturgy is thus the outstanding means by which the faithful can express in their lives, and manifest to others, the mystery of Christ and the real nature of the true Church (Preamble, 2).

He [Christ] is present in the sacrifice of the Mass, not only in the person of His minister, "the same one now offering, through the ministry of priests, who formerly offered himself on the cross," but especially under the Eucharistic species (I, 7).

In the earthly liturgy, by way of foretaste, we share in that heavenly liturgy which is celebrated in the holy city of Jerusalem toward which we journey as pilgrims, and in which Christ is sitting at the right hand of God . . . (I, 8).

Popular devotions of the Christian people are warmly recommended, provided they are in accord with the laws and norms of the Church. Such is especially the case with devotions called for by the Apostolic See (I, 13).

Regulation of the sacred liturgy depends solely on the authority of the Church, that is, on the Apostolic See and, as laws may determine, on the bishop (III, 22, #1).

Therefore, absolutely no other person, not even a priest, may add, remove, or change anything in the liturgy on his own authority (III, 22, #3).

The saints have been traditionally honored in the Church and their authentic relics and images held in veneration. For the feasts of the saints proclaim the wonderful works of Christ in His servants, and display to the faithful fitting examples for their imitation (V, 111).

The Church acknowledges Gregorian chant as proper to the Roman liturgy: therefore, other things being equal, it should be given pride of place in liturgical services (VI, 116).

In the Latin Church the pipe organ is to be held in high esteem, for it is the traditional musical instrument, and one that adds a wonderful splendor to the Church's ceremonies and powerfully lifts up man's mind to God and to heavenly things (VI, 120).

Ordinaries must be very careful to see that sacred furnishings and works of value are not disposed of or allowed to deteriorate; for they are the ornaments of the house of God (VII, 126).[1]

Cautious departures from standard customs were permitted in the document, but even in dealing with the question of the vernacular liturgy the Council fathers seemed to envision translation as exceptional, Latin as normal (III, 36, #3).

The great paradox of Catholic reform in the 1960s was the fact that those who were least happy with the changes, and who became most disaffected from the Church, were those who had striven hardest to bring the changes about. Less than two years after the Council ended, one of the leading American liturgists, the Benedictine Godfrey Diekmann, for many years editor of *Worship*, asked, "Are we too late?" Citing the opinions of the liberal Baptist theologian Harvey Cox, the liberal Anglican bishop John Robinson, and the popular folksinger Joan Baez, he speculated that even the reformed liturgy had little meaning for contemporary man. Perhaps the changes had been to no avail.[2]

Harvey Cox's work *The Secular City*, probably the most

influential religious book of the decade, had appeared in 1965, and liturgists and theologians were not slow in assimilating its thesis—that contemporary man is content to live in a secularized world, in accordance with a pragmatic ethic, unconcerned about "ultimate reality," interested only in improving the world. In such a context liturgy could obviously have little meaning unless drastically revised.

Rather precociously a lay woman had already, several years before, pointed out certain problems which liturgical reformers acknowledged only dimly—that much of the liturgy is archaic and dependent on a sacramental sense of nature and the cosmos which modern man either does not possess or can acquire only with difficulty. Liturgists, she suggested, were trying to build worship on an attitude toward the universe which is largely foreign to modern man. The priest-sociologist Andrew Greeley responded that modern man's sense of transcendence and apprehension of the sacred are stronger than Mary Perkins Ryan recognized, that man would in fact keep returning to his need for ritual and worship.[3] The debate ended temporarily, only to burst out in full force soon after the liturgical reforms of the Council had been implemented.

As the Council opened, Louis Bouyer had warned against two dangers besetting the liturgists: taking refuge in an immobile traditionalism, in which liturgy would petrify; and rejecting altogether the domain of the sacred, the force of tradition, and the sense of reverence, in the name of a spurious purity.[4] The actions of the Council rendered the former impossible, except among small groups which soon became openly schismatic. The uncertainties of the time, however, guaranteed that the latter course would have strong appeal. What was surprising was that it encountered so little opposition, except among relatively untutored and unsophisticated people.

Early in the fateful year 1966 a Benedictine monk articulated the new spirit: worship was to be characterized above all by spontaneity; he suggested that a successful Mass might be one which generated "the fun of a successful cocktail party." [5] A Lutheran architect, taking his inspiration from the German theologian Dietrich Bonhoeffer, urged that designers of churches "deal unabashedly with the finite, the ordinary, the secular, the everyday, the contemporary, the particular. And he ought to avoid . . . all those temptations to make of a church something different, special, or 'religious.'" [6] A Jesuit characterized traditional liturgy as a breeding ground for atheism, because it seemed to make God irrelevant to life.[7] A retreat master proclaimed that "the retreat is no time for long faces and frowning concentration." [8] The abbot primate of the Benedictines suggested that worship is no longer to convey "a feeling of infinity or eternity or the world beyond—an experience of man approaching God that is unique to that moment," which would lead to "a new archaism and a neo-archaeologism," but "is to be primarily the communal sensitivity that I am one with my brother next to me and that our song is our common twentieth-century situation. . . ." He urged that sacred music "deny her exalted position of being a 'telephone to the beyond.'" [9]

At the 1966 Liturgical Week in Houston, Texas, a Jesuit theologian expounded with conviction Harvey Cox's thesis about secularity and warned that worship could be a form of escape from the demands of social justice. Mary Perkins Ryan lamented that the Eucharist was still not fully recognizable for what it is—a community meal. Cautiously she suggested that other elements besides bread and wine might be used. A parish priest on the board of the Liturgical Conference said he found the exuberance of amateur skaters at Rockefeller Center more truly liturgical than Mass in a

nearby church. He noted, however, that the spirit of celebration cannot be sustained indefinitely and pointed to the
bullfight as an outstanding ritual celebration.[10]

Although such ideas represented a radical departure
from the spirit and goals of the Liturgical Movement prior
to the Council, they were not much debated and by the end
of 1966 seem to have compelled general assent among liturgists, although there were commanders and foot soldiers
from the earlier wars who saw that the new conflict was not
theirs and dropped out. By early 1967 a new editor of *Worship* admitted that the relationship of the sacred and the
secular was a crucial one for the liturgy but thought it could
be dealt with by recognizing that "contemporary man does
not deny the transcendental, but he seeks it within the life
of this world. . . . There is no hope for a liturgical reform
which would equate the secular with the profane." He was
appalled at the state of the religious arts and thought most
theaters and museums were better expressions of the sacred
than contemporary church buildings.[11] A British composer
urged that all music of the past be banished from the
churches and relegated to the concert halls,[12] and the abbot
primate of the Benedictines complained that the Divine
Office was too "God-centered and vertical." [13] The editor
of *Worship* wondered why liturgists could not learn from
American civic pageantry how to construct relevant liturgies;
the President, for example, does not wear special vestments
at his inauguration, and chanting is clearly out of place in
American culture. Since the rest of the world seems destined
to become Americanized, he thought liturgies built on the
American model would gradually come to have wide usefulness.[14]

In 1969 the General Secretariate of Concilium, an influential group of European theologians, rejected the " 'mythical'
symbols which lend a magic superstitious character to public
prayer and devotion, the unhealthy climate of escapist

dreams." They called for "the symbols of a freedom which creates its own forms, its own interhuman dialogue where man represents God and finds his image of God." A Spanish Benedictine, writing in a Concilium volume on liturgy, contemptuously dismissed all the "archaic" and "meaningless" trappings of worship and warned that it created the "practicing type" of Catholic rather than the "believing type." The former was characterized as living in fear, unfree, compulsively searching for security, guilty of "the sin of magic," while the latter type seeks by free and personal efforts to create "a more just world." An Italian composer heaped praises on the youth Masses in which "one expresses oneself and realizes oneself" and dismissed the organ as expressive of "a decidedly senile spirituality." Concerning traditional worship he said that "Only a god of the dead could be pleased with such glacial homage and the faithful who do not rebel on seeing the communitary [sic] enclosed in such a funereal apparatus probably believe not in the God of rites but in the rites themselves." [15]

Against all this, relatively few authoritative voices were raised. One of the most eloquent was the Anglican theologian John Macquarrie, who recognized a great crisis of faith and not simply a controversy over the forms of worship.[16] Dietrich von Hildebrand, a layman who had written perceptively about liturgy for many years, warned about the *Trojan Horse in the City of God.* Jacques Maritain, the principal intellectual mentor of two generations of Catholic reformers, expressed profound misgivings in the voice of *The Peasant of the Garonne.* Louis Bouyer dissected *The Decomposition of Catholicism.* For the most part, however, such attitudes were dismissed as merely reactionary. Little effort was made to extract what was valid from these critiques.

The liturgical revolution which occurred with such remarkable speed in a year's time left liturgists in an anomalous situation, however. Once the principle had been accepted that liturgy should be relevant in a secular way, cutting itself off from the world in no significant manner, deliberately modern, and as far as possible spontaneous and expressive of personal feelings, it was clear that the established liturgy, even as reformed by the Council and assuming further changes in the proximate future, was not very usable. All inheritances from the past, all set prayers and gestures, all prescribed forms were more or less arbitrary, and insofar as they still had relevance it had to be tested in each case. In a sense the official liturgy was to be considered guilty until proved innocent.

The editor of *Worship* asserted that nothing in the liturgy was necessarily fixed, including the words of institution or consecration, "if the liturgy is normally self-expression of the Christian community. . . ." When reports circulated about unauthorized experiments conducted in hotel rooms at the Houston Liturgical Week of 1966, he pointed out that they were not sponsored by the Liturgical Conference, but also warned that more such experiments would be forthcoming unless official reforms were sufficiently "radical (in the good sense) to make the liturgy fully relevant for today." By 1968 the Liturgical Conference had largely cut its ties to Church authorities and conducted the Washington Liturgical Week on the subject of "Revolution," with a succession of speakers on economic and political topics. *Worship's* attitude remained mildly approving.[17]

The search for relevant liturgy, however, soon began to suffer from the Harvey Cox syndrome—a fundamental uncertainty about precisely who "secular man" is and for what he is searching. The complacently pragmatic and optimistic spirit of the New Frontier and the Great Society began to give way to more frequent and more obvious manifestations of *Angst*, identity problems, and the search for meaning, all of which seemed to lead away from pragmatism and politics and back into the soul, to the spiritual life, to metaphysics, even to ritual. The Harvey Cox who in 1965 had considered "technopolitan man" perhaps the highest achievement of civilization was longing by 1971 to be "like the Cheyenne— in touch with the seasons and the animals in the sky. . . . But it is beyond our grasp, perhaps forever. . . . And now we sit, if not quite in the funeral parlor, then in the sterilized geriatric ward, remembering—and wishing it could have been different." [18] Professor Cox did not remain despairing for long, however, and soon countered *The Secular City* with *Feast of Fools*. The counter-culture emerged as an infatuation with fantasy, play, ritual, archaic roots, even hallucination, in full retreat from the disciplined, almost puritanical political activism of the middle 1960s. The problems of creating relevant liturgy in such confused and unstable times became almost insurmountable, although heroic efforts were made by numerous individuals.

In the process, not surprisingly, some of those most intimately involved in the struggle concluded that the effort was fruitless and essentially meaningless. The lay executive secretary of the Liturgical Conference, who had put forward a rather conservative and balanced program in 1963, revealed a decade later that "I couldn't care less. The urgent cause of liturgical reform which meant so much to me then means nothing to me now. Since the summer's end of 1967, the church has faded from my consciousness much as my years in the Army have." He had discovered, he wrote, that Christianity is not unique and that at the heart of all religions are a few humanistic concepts, beside which "the supernatural elements become less interesting." And furthermore: "The demythologized core of religion turns out to be human nature. The God of my youth was created by men." [19] His successor at the Liturgical Conference, also a layman, urged while in office that "Worship is a word religion should try to forget" and "the entire meaning of the liturgy can be summed up with precision in one word—empathy." After leaving the Conference he became an adviser to Gamemasters Inc. on the marketing of the "Jesus deck," a card game similar to gin rummy in which the winner shouts, "Witness!" and reads an inspirational quote from the cards.[20] The Liturgical Weeks, held since 1940 and at their peak capable of attracting twenty thousand people to St. Louis in 1964, were canceled following the Milwaukee week of 1969. The program had become more and more radical and secular, and there was a drastic falling off in attendance.

Still, many persons of great sincerity, learning, and energy remained interested in liturgy, trying a variety of approaches toward constructing "a worship for modern man." The Liturgical Movement had, however, for better or for worse entered a new phase which was not simply an extension or advance on its previous character but, in certain crucial ways, a denial and a repudiation of its earlier self, the self which had inspired and brought to fruition such notable changes in the Church's manner of worship. Among the principal differences were: (1) Rather than a desire to change the liturgy in order to show forth the "sacred mysteries" more effectively, it manifested deep suspicion of the mystical character of worship as a distraction from human problems. (2) Rather than emphasizing the timeless and perennially valid forms of the liturgy, it sought to bring it as much as possible into conformity with contemporary culture. (3) From a relationship of fundamental respect and obedience to Church authorities, it began to conceive its role increasingly as one of divergence from officially prescribed forms. (4) From seeking forms of worship valid for the whole Church, it came to a preoccupation with liturgies usable only by special groups and an eager acceptance of the notion of "liturgical pluralism."

NOTES

1. All quotations from *Constitution on the Sacred Liturgy* are from the translation of Msgr. Joseph Gallagher in *The Documents of Vatican II*, ed. Walter M. Abbott, S.J. (New York, 1966), pp. 137–78.

2. "The Reform of Catholic Liturgy: Are We Too Late?" *Worship*, XLI, 3 (March, 1967), pp. 142–51.

3. Ryan, "The Problem of God in the World Today," *Worship*, XXXIV, 1 (December, 1959), pp. 9–19, and "The Psychology of Worship: Another Approach," *Worship*, XXXIV, 7 (June–July, 1960), pp. 380–6. Greeley, "Psychology of Worship," *Worship*, XXXIV, 4 (March, 1960), pp. 188–95.

4. "Two Temptations," *Worship*, XXXVII, 1 (December, 1962), pp. 11–21.

5. Colman Grabert, O.S.B., "Toward the Development of an Authentic English Sung Mass," *Worship*, XL, 2 (February, 1966), pp. 80–90.

6. Edward A. Sövick, "The Architecture of Kerygma," *Worship*, XL, 4 (April, 1966), pp. 196–208.

7. John J. Gallen, S.J., "Liturgical Atheism," *Worship*, XL, 7 (August–September, 1966), pp. 430–36.

8. David B. Wadhams, S.M., "Towards a Renewed Retreat Theology," *Worship*, XL, 9 (November, 1966), pp. 584–88.

9. Rembert Weakland, O.S.B., "Music as Art in Liturgy," *Worship*, XLI, 1 (January, 1967), pp. 5–15.

10. Daniel O'Hanlon, S.J., Mary Perkins Ryan, and John DeWitt in *Worship in the City of Man* (The Liturgical Conference, 1966), pp. 16–38, 150–58.

11. Aelred Tegels, O.S.B., *Worship*, XLI, 2 (February, 1967), p. 117.

12. Anthony Milner, "The Instruction on Sacred Music," *Worship*, XLI, 6 (May, 1967), pp. 322–33.

13. Weakland, "The Divine Office and Contemporary Man," *Worship*, XLIII, 4 (April, 1969), pp. 214–18.

14. Tegels, "Liturgy and Culture: Adaptation or Symbiosis?" *Worship*, XLI, 6 (June–July, 1967), pp. 364–72.

15. Concilium General Secretariate: Evangelista Vilanova, O.S.B., and Gino Stefani in *The Crisis of Liturgical Reform* (*Concilium*, XLII [1969]), pp. 6–19, 71–86, 174–80.

16. "Subjectivity and Objectivity in Theology and Worship," *Worship*, XLI, 3 (March, 1967), pp. 152–60.

17. Tegels, "Liturgy and Culture," p. 366; *Worship*, XL, 9 (November, 1966), p. 589, and XLII, 8 (October, 1968), p. 502.

18. "Jack Crabb—Antiheroic Everyman," *The National Catholic Reporter*, March 18, 1971, p. 11.

19. John B. Mannion, "The Making of a Dissident," *Commonweal*, January 19, 1973, pp. 344–46.

20. James Colaianni, *The Catholic Left* (Philadelphia, 1968), pp. 26–27. Colaianni's connection with the "Jesus deck" is reported by John Deedy, *Commonweal*, March 23, 1973, p. 50.

CHAPTER 2

The Chimera of Relevance

Prior to the 1960s the Liturgical Movement, insofar as it went beyond a preoccupation with liturgy in the narrowest sense, grounded itself not only in the depths of orthodox Catholic theology but also in the work of certain scholarly students of religious phenomena whose position was essentially humanistic but who pointed to the "religious sense" in man as an ineradicable and central part of human life.

The seminal study was of *The Idea of the Holy* by the German historian of religion Rudolf Otto, who analyzed man's recurring fascination with "the wholly other"—some reality or power beyond all human categories, capable of inspiring both dread and attraction, a reality toward which only attitudes of reverence, awe, wonder, and even fear are appropriate. In Christianity, however, Otto saw a crucial metamorphosis in this religious sense—the Wholly Other is perceived as the God of three persons, and the Son inspires love and free human response. The Christian religion is thus necessarily built on a tension between the Son of God become man and the continuing awareness of a divine reality far above all human experience.

The Romanian anthropologist Mircea Eliade dichotomized

The Sacred and the Profane, which he saw as opposed categories in almost all human cultures. The sacred, deliberately fenced off from the merely worldly, represents the fullness of being, the basic ordering of the universe, the bulwark against chaos. Paradoxically, it alone makes human life possible, since in a wholly profane world man lives in constant danger of slipping back into a formless, chaotic existence. Insofar as modern man has lost his awareness of the sacred, Eliade viewed this as an impoverishment of human life, to be deplored and if possible reversed.

The thrust of liturgical reform was, prior to the Second Vatican Council, primarily toward a powerful restatement of the importance of the sacred. The principal criticism which liturgists made of the Mass as actually celebrated was that, in too many parishes, it was "said" quickly, sloppily, irreverently, as a duty to be performed rather than a divine mystery to be entered into. Popular nonliturgical devotions were disapproved because they tended to detract from the central importance of the Eucharist and because they so often stalled on the superficial level of petition and thanksgiving for favors rather than leading the participants to a full knowledge of the mystery of redemption. Not all liturgists favored the vernacular, but those who did expected that a deep reverence and sense of awe could be preserved even in translation.

The liturgical revolution of the later 1960s rejected, sometimes sharply and even stridently, the traditional belief that worship points to a world "beyond," that it focuses man's attention on a transcendent God, that it is the act whereby man elevates himself "above" the mundane world in order to glimpse the source from which he came and the goal toward which he moves. The "theology of Incarnation" began to assert that God is found in the world itself, and only there, and that aspirations toward transcendence, as understood traditionally in the Church, are in fact heretical and antihuman. A French Dominican theologian urged the deliberate "desacralization" of worship, since it had been found that sacred beliefs are difficult to adjust to cultural change.[1] A German Jesuit liturgist hailed man's losing his "childish enthusiasms." With vehemence he asserted that "Radical desacralization is necessary. . . . and that includes the casting down of idols and sanctuaries. . . ." Liturgical reform aimed to free man from "sacral hocus pocus." (The term "hocus pocus" is thought to derive from a puritan jibe at the Latin words of consecration, *Hoc est enim Corpus Meum.* The ready acceptance of this deliberate blasphemy of a modern liturgist indicates how deeply the puritan spirit has taken root, even if unrecognized.) The same priest scorned all warnings against secularization, since the fruit of that process was likely to be a wholly benign purification by religious beliefs and practices. The new liturgy would require no special vestments, rubrics, or other trappings of the sacred. An Anglican priest pronounced the language of the Book of Common Prayer inappropriate to modern worship because it reflects too "other-worldly" a religion, is too majestic and "poetic" in its tones. A Spanish priest-liturgist welcomed secularization as a means of countering the "magic" and "arrogance" of traditional worship. There is, he thought, "enormous gain for the purity of the liturgy" in attacks from skeptics and secularists, because liturgy will no longer be able to distract man from the world and "will have something to say for men of today." [2]

General consensus about the need for a worldly mode of worship could not, however, translate itself immediately into "relevant" liturgy, especially since even the reformed rite of the Second Vatican Council is fundamentally traditional and obviously based on the classic conception of the function of worship. The prayers are addressed to the Father directly, through Christ, and there is little which has any direct bearing on contemporary human problems. The "ex-

perimental liturgies" which first began to attract attention at
the Liturgical Week of 1966 now became bolder and far
more common; soon no city of any size and scarcely any
Catholic college were without experimental groups. An
ironically well-publicized "underground church" began to
surface, and numerous church members, dissatisfied with
the irrelevance of regular Sunday worship, left the parishes
to join these new groups. Soon it was clear that the crisis
of relevance, and the crisis of worship which was an aspect of
it, was not confined to one denomination; disaffected "modern Christians" began to have ecumenical encounters amid
liturgies in each other's living rooms.

Underground liturgies, or more precisely liturgies devised
with no particular regard for the official liturgies of the
Church, remain a feature of contemporary religious life. But
from the beginning the search for a truly modern form of
worship was plagued by certain internal contradictions
which are probably inescapable. Of these the most fundamental is the fact that Christian worship has always been
structured for the most part "vertically"—man calling upon
God, glorifying Him, thanking Him, asking His blessing,
with only a rather formal and generalized attention to human
needs, the relation of the worshipers to one another treated
as an adjunct to their preoccupation with God. In liturgies
of the classic pattern, even those of quite recent vintage like
the reformed rites of the Roman Church or the *Services for
Trial Use* of the Episcopal Church, the celebrant addresses
the worshipers only sparingly and the worshipers address
each other scarcely at all. The search for a liturgy which
is primarily "horizontal"—focused on the community itself
and on God within other people—is necessarily a profound
break with the whole worshiping tradition of the Church
and calls into question the very idea of worship, not simply
the specific forms of it currently in official use.

Classically, worship has been conceived as relating to a

special "divine life" accessible to man, either through the sacramental action itself (as in Catholicism) or through a special divine action which the sacraments symbolize and proclaim (as in Protestantism). In the new theology, however, man is conceived as having no "grace" which is distinct from "nature," and the purpose of worship and sacraments is to illumine all of natural human life and to celebrate human victories over all that is destructive and tyrannical.[3] In such an economy, the very need for and possibility of worship become problematical, since life itself manifests God fully and special religious acts tend to express a traditional misunderstanding about the nature of salvation. The notion that a "successful" Mass is like a successful cocktail party, or that exuberant skaters and dedicated bull fighters are creating more authentic liturgies than the Church, may seem like the unavoidable absurdities of a fringe of enthusiasts. Yet a certain logic attaches to such positions. If, in worshiping, man is primarily celebrating the goodness of God's creation and the discovery of Him in other men, then the natural human moments of insight, exhilaration, and celebration—parties, games, intimate conversations—are in fact truer liturgies than anything consciously devised, no matter how "radical." There appears to be no need for organized liturgies when true human celebrations occur more or less spontaneously all the time. The failure to recognize this ultimate implication of the theology of secularity was a trap which doomed the search for relevant liturgy almost from the beginning.

It was an insight which slowly dawned on a number of people. A former secretary of the Liturgical Conference recalls that

. . . since "liturgy is the school of Christian formation" . . . , what better place to start the reformation of the world than in the rites of Catholic worship? . . . I was enrolled for seven or eight years.

My later doubts were born of impatience and frustration. I began to think that maybe the theory is right but it sure as hell is a slow way to deliver aid to the world. Maybe it would be better to work directly on the problems of the day than to go by way of Rome. Of such thoughts are dropouts made.[4]

A New Jersey priest who became the leader of an underground church reported that his community found that simple livingroom Eucharists with guitars, baker's bread, and drugstore wine quickly lost their meaning. Social action alone seemed important.[5] There are no statistics, but in all probability very few of the underground liturgical groups begun with such hopes and enthusiasms in the later 1960s survived for any length of time. There were many reasons for this, but perhaps most important was ultimate realization by so many participants that the logic of their belief dictated an essentially secular existence. The regular celebration of liturgies came to seem like an arbitrary concession to tradition, a bit of "churchiness" anomalously held onto amid general emancipation from the ecclesiastical establishment.

The Harvey Cox syndrome was also at the heart of the search for relevance, since it proved to be extraordinarily difficult to judge with any degree of accuracy what was or was not truly relevant to "the world." Experimentation with the liturgy began in the era when "social problems," primarily economic and political, still held the center of attention, and the proper stance of a committed human being seemed to be one of clear-eyed, determined, informed, and pragmatic idealism. The mood was puritanical, as the activist began systematically shedding excess baggage, material and spiritual luxuries (was not prayer a distraction from worldly tasks?), and preparing for battles to be fought on the campaign trail, on picket lines, and in a multitude of public and private social agencies. In such a context meaningful liturgy seemed to require ordinary secular dress, a minimum of ritual and ceremony, readings from the daily newspapers of current books on social injustice, and "dialogue homilies" about how to cope with problems in the surrounding community.

Progressive clergy shed their vestments on the sacristy floor, threw their incense in the trash, and sold their golden vessels to antique dealers, only to discover that somehow the puritanical young men and women who had marched with them on the picket lines had got hold of all these discards and more besides—tarot cards, Ouija boards, Tibetan prayer wheels, and temple gongs. The Latin had been eliminated from the Mass so the young could comprehend it, but they preferred instead to chant in Sanskrit. Campus chaplains had ceased trying to sell prayer and were selling social action instead, but their former constituents were hunting up Hindu gurus and undertaking systematic regimens of meditation and fasting. Some clergy lectured the Church severely about the evil of sacral liturgies which are "escapes from life," but the young increasingly preferred drug-induced euphoria and hallucinations.

On one level this confusion over what was truly worldly stemmed from a simple and relatively harmless error: being mostly rather unworldly themselves, liturgical reformers knew no better way to overcome this disadvantage than by following the lead of the youth culture, which appeared to represent whatever was most modern. They failed to notice, until much later, the degree to which that culture was fragmented, unstable, and immensely subject to fad and caprice, so that almost any program which sought to relate to it was doomed to obsolescence by the time it was even properly organized.

On another level, more serious, the Cox syndrome laid bare the profound confusion of so many reformers themselves and their profound uncertainty as to what it meant to be modern, how susceptible they themselves were to fads and to violent swings of the pendulum. The Church was under attack from both sides, but as it turned out the same guerrillas were fighting on both the right and the left. Harvey Cox first castigated the establishment for its refusal to grow up, its penchant for myths and comforting legends, then for its stodgy lack of imagination, its failure to recognize the importance of fantasy and ritual celebration. The Episcopal bishop James A. Pike of California first defiantly said in *If This Be Heresy* that modern scientific man cannot accept legendary teachings like the Virgin Birth, then came to be an ardent believer in Spiritualism. Modernizers soon revealed their deep uncertainty whether "reality" is that everyday life apprehended by common sense, or something far beyond normal experience. It is impossible, however, to create liturgy which is simultaneously relevant to both.

On the deepest level such uncertainties demonstrated a general failure to consider what relevance actually is or what the world is which liturgy is to be made relevant to. "The world" and "modern man" came to be generalized abstractions applicable at best to specialized segments of reality, which were willfully mistaken for the whole. There was little reflection on the fact that probably the majority of people in the world—the masses of Asia, Africa, and Latin America, for example, as well as many in the more "advanced" cultures —are "religious" people in the pejorative sense of the term used by Bonhoeffer and the secularizing theologians. Paradoxically, the judgment that modern man is inevitably secular is possible only on the assumption that the forms and values of the Western industrial societies are fated to overwhelm the whole world and that *they should;* few progressive churchmen are prepared to accept that dogma, however. Among the most common "human needs" is the desire for stability, tradition, and order, yet few experimental liturgies seek to fulfill this need, and neglecting to do so they often prove to be dysfunctional.

The necessity of a desacralized, "worldly" form of worship has been generally justified as historical—secularization is occurring, there is no possibility of preventing it, its blessings should be gladly accepted. But if secularization is in fact a historical inevitability, there is little need to work and plan for it; it will occur in good time, and a properly secularized worship will evolve naturally. If it is not inevitable, then Christians have the duty and the power to choose whether to accept or resist it; the attempt to impose secularization as inevitable is a suppression of Christian and human freedom.

The inevitability of secularization, and the necessary irrelevance of stable and sacral worship, has been repeatedly urged on the grounds that contemporary man lives in a constantly changing world in which there is little continuity with the past and much awareness of continuous and disruptive change. To be truly modern, in this view, is to cease looking for stabilities and certainties and to live at ease in an insecure environment. There is truth in this reading of history, mainly to the extent that this is now a cultural condition which many people wish to see come about and have chosen to promote in various ways. To the degree that it appeals to historical forces beyond human control it is greatly exaggerated, however. Sudden and violent change has been the familiar lot of Western man at least since the time of the Black Death more than six hundred years ago, and succeeding ages have lived through fundamental changes like the breakup of the feudal system, the Reformation, the religious wars, the Scientific Revolution, the Industrial Revolution, and the two world wars. Even the force of technology, which appears to strike the present age particularly hard, was experienced perhaps at least as powerfully by the men of the early nineteenth century who saw the first factories, locomotives, and steamships and the men of the early twentieth who witnessed the advent of airplanes, automobiles, motion pictures, and machine guns. What is least convincing in the argument from historical change is its failure to explain why man should be apparently so much more secular in 1970 than in 1960, 1950, or 1940, when traditional religion seemed to be in as healthy a condition as it had been for a long time.

It is also paradoxical that some of those individuals who were among the earliest and most acute diagnosticians of what it means to be modern, who helped articulate the ideas which now flow so easily from theologians' pens, responded to "modernity" precisely by recognizing the continued, indeed intensified, importance of traditional religion. T. S. Eliot and W. H. Auden not only joined the Church of England but opposed most of the modernizing tendencies within it. Of the composer Igor Stravinsky, a Russian Orthodox, his closest associate has said:

He believed in the Devil Incarnate, and in a literal, Dantesque Hell, Purgatory, and Paradise. And he was deeply superstitious, forever crossing himself and those around him, wearing sacred medals, [a footnote indicates a special devotion to Our Lady of Perpetual Help,] and performing compulsive acts without which the auguries for the day were certain to be unfavorable. Furthermore, he believed in miracles, both large and of the Houdini sort, and never questioned the provenance of any sacred relic. Dogmatism was another part of his religion. . . .[6]

Such men belonged to an earlier generation of Western seers but, except for the fact that it was not primarily Christian, there was a similar religious revival occurring among avant-garde young people by the end of the 1960s. What most of these converts appear to have seen in Catholicism, and what many other intellectuals have sought for and found in other places besides the Church, is precisely some reality or vision which is not modern. They have made the judgment that modern culture, in its secularity, is radically truncated, lacking in some awareness of reality which most societies of the past possessed and many in the present still possess. No secular man celebrates secularity with the enthusiasm of progressive theologians. Insofar as the Church chooses to show its essentially worldly side to the world, whether this be simple love of power and wealth or a principled hankering after modernity, it loses all claim to attention, since it is reduced simply to telling the world what the world already knows, and for the most part telling it badly.

The search for relevance suffered in part because there was never any clear idea what motivated it. If the primary motivation was to impress secular men with the need to take the Church seriously, it has been a dismal failure. Irving Howe probably speaks for many in the intellectual world when he says:

Consider the new wave of social consciousness among Catholics and Protestants alike: whatever its political value, isn't it clear that many of its adherents are people who have lost the religious substance yet retain a core of religious yearning? Isn't it clear, as well, that for many of these people, good and sincere as they may be, the religious symbols and vocabularies have become little more than enabling cues for the secular passions which are their real concern? [7]

If the search was primarily motivated by a desire to keep in the Church people who might otherwise leave, it has been at best a partial success, since changes in traditional structure have proved to be somewhat like giving a thirsty man salt water to drink—they merely induce a craving for more.

T. S. Eliot once wrote that although Christianity always modifies itself so as to remain believable in each age, conscious attempts to achieve this, like Modernism, "always have the opposite effect." [8] The explanation of the paradox is not difficult—deliberate and well-publicized "reforms" can easily come to seem like desperate acts by people who have at last come to realize that they occupy uninhabitable territory and are making one final effort to improve the property before abandoning it. If the Church was so badly wrong on so many questions for so many centuries, there is little reason to take it seriously now, admirable though its honest professions of error may be.

This pseudo-relevance crept into liturgy as priests readily allowed the sacred rites to be stretched, bent, and broken to accommodate the momentary tastes of particular groups, whether serious or whimsical. The most notorious cases were the coffee-and-doughnut or beer-and-pretzel Eucharists, the gatherings where *agape* moved aside to admit *eros*, and the groups who used marijuana to stimulate "religious experiences." Perhaps almost as deadly, however, were the many cases in which the established structure of the Mass all but disappeared under the hand of eager experimenters or where the Eucharist became so relevant to worldly problems as to lose almost all sacral character. Whatever value such gatherings may have had for their participants, they sought to make liturgy relevant by in effect killing it. Many participants appear to have been purged by such experiences; they emerged to discover that they no longer had any need to join in a religious rite. Others discovered a simple truth: it is easier to become inspired for social action by attending a political rally, reading a graphic account of injustice, or visiting the scenes of need than by attempting to secularize an essentially sacred rite. In making the liturgy relevant many clergy unwittingly demonstrated merely its ultimate poverty in any framework of belief they or their special congregations could accept. Curiously, avant-garde liturgies seem for the most part to attract mainly those from within the Church who are experiencing some kind of faith crisis, many of whom finally leave; there is little indication that they have attracted any large number of seekers from the outside.

The Anglican dean Ralph Inge once commented that "He who marries the spirit of the age is soon left a widower," and perhaps the greatest irony of the search for relevance is the fact that nothing so quickly becomes irrelevant as that which seemed intensely relevant only a short time before. It is the clothes, films, and fond illusions of the generation just prior to the present which usually seem most ludicrous; the modernists of the 1960s judged the 1950s as one of the dreariest of decades, and many of the passions of the 1960s already seem ridiculous. The proposal to model liturgy after the presidential inauguration ceremony may have seemed promising in 1967, but by early 1969 the avant-garde was holding "counter-inaugurals" which sought to discredit the official ceremony by ridicule. The modernists of 1970 hardly had much respect for the bland, businesslike character of official American ceremonial. (The monk who so admired the ceremony of inauguration did not perhaps attend to its roots in a puritan distrust of all ritual, which is scarcely compatible with Catholic liturgy.)

At the Liturgical Week in Seattle in 1962 a priest-liturgist narrated a demonstration of a promising new way of making ritual relevant: at the Offertory selected members of the congregation would come forward not merely with bread and wine but also with appropriate symbols of their worldly occupations. It was a rite which would be tried in a number of places in the years to come, but without engendering much enthusiasm. (Among other problems was the anomaly by which the donors would reclaim, after the Mass, the gifts they had "given" at the Offertory.) As each donor came forward the priest commented:

Women are not only cooks, they are housewives. . . . Along with the dustcloth she has a skirt, a man's shirt, neatly pressed and ironed. . . . I'm sure it often seems an undramatic and weary way to heaven. But what does it matter as long as it *is* a way to heaven, a way to serve each other in the name of Christ?

The nun has another book in her hand, the book of her holy rule. And it isn't the book but all the acts of holy obedience that she leaves upon the altar. Obedience is a difficult virtue, especially for the young. (But we might think of Christ and Mary: Your redemption depended on their obedience. And the redemption of so many more might depend on yours.)

. . . the jets that have made the world ever more one community, and the bombers which brave men are using right now to keep vigil, so we can meet and talk and pray. . . .

. . . there are a good many lessons of discipline and obedience, bitter disappointments, and clean, hard sportsmanship that you can offer to God—if you accept them first—acts of humility, too, when the [football] coach tells you off.[9]

The unfortunate creator of this rite could not have foretold that in less than five years' time his carefully thought-out ceremony would come to seem to many people not, perhaps, irrelevant but actually pernicious. He could not have foreseen Women's Liberation, the revolution in the religious life, the antiwar movement, or a widespread rejection among young people of the ethos of football and the dictatorial authority of the coach. Catholic cardinals have sometimes been criticized for blessing bombers; being liturgical traditionalists, however, they never thought of putting model bombers on the altar. A liturgy which appears strikingly relevant at one moment is likely for that very reason to be monumentally irrelevant much sooner than a liturgy which has retained its appeal across the years. A truly contemporary liturgy is one which demands to be completely redrawn at least every five years, to catch shifts in national mood, changing political issues, new forms of speech replacing older ones (slang, for example, tends to have a short life), and oscillating taste in art. (Artists and architects who insisted on a severe functional style in the early 1960s, for example, did not foresee the revived love of extravagant decoration which would be inspired by the counter-culture.) If liturgy is wholly spontaneous and created by each congregation for its own use, this might be possible, although it is likely to exceed the creative powers of most groups. As a liturgical strategy for the whole Church it is patently impossible. The modern experience of worship seems also to confirm that the most objectionable aspects of liturgy are precisely those things which were introduced as concessions to the secular spirit of a particular age, for example, the etiquette of baroque monarchy or the sentimentalities of Romantic piety.

The struggle to achieve a truly relevant liturgy, and the notion that worship does not relate specifically to divine life in man but is, rather, a celebration of all human life, leads inexorably to the secularization of liturgy, to a situation in which the ritual of the Church ceases in fact to be Christian except in the vaguest sense. Relevance is achieved by systematically eliminating, or allowing to be obscured, the distinctively religious aspects of worship in favor of a merely human activity.

Thus the priest who devised so relevant an Offertory in 1962 was, a decade later, discovering that "making the Eucharist" is simply "to make the ordinary suddenly extraordinary, and to give thanks with bread and wine and people where you find them. . . ." The term "Sacrifice of the Mass" is deemed no longer useful because worship is now recognized as "an important human act." (Sacrifice is a concept retaining limited value because of "people like Jesus and Gandhi who freely choose a course involving risk.") The essence of worship is defined as follows:

If you can speak of a relationship between infinite force and fragile men in which our person and potential are so highly valued that force can be described as Father and man as God's son, this is good news indeed. And it deserves an unambiguous shout to declare it, not a lot of talk about a propitiatory sacrifice to bring it about.

Christ's discourse about eating His body and drinking His blood is compared to a mother's saying to her child. "I could eat you up!" and the Communion is described as "sharing one bread we call his body. . . ." A proposal is endorsed to transform churches into centers for "the arts *in* celebration," and the continued importance of the Mass is argued on the grounds that it is "a symbol of ultimacy, that which endures when the sounds are silent. . . . there is nothing else in Western culture, and certainly not in our own religious tradition, which expresses more enduringly the victory of life and the hope of man than does the mass." [10] Whether intended or not, this is an approach to liturgy which easily reduces it to a metaphor for various human experiences, and in which religious faith is not a necessary ingredient.

So also a monastic press can produce a poster, suitable for use on chapel walls, which proclaims a frankly profane slogan like "Nothing is worth more than this day." A priest can suggest that family vacations be considered true sacraments insofar as they refresh people and make them more open to one another and to God.[11] The last stage of trying to save liturgy from obsolescence is inevitably to humanize it to the point where it is not substantially different from any number of human actions. Paradoxically, at this point the validity of worship becomes more problematical, not less, since the use of Christian formulas comes to seem arbitrary and provincial if they are intended to express universal human experiences. Why, for example, should the Eucharist be conceded such central importance? Left to himself, modern man would not be likely to designate a meal of bread and wine as his central symbol of unity. If the sacraments celebrate life, there are more authentic ways of celebrating than in ecclesiastical rituals—at parties, dances, sporting events, concerts, or dinners with friends. (A sympathetic observer of the Dutch Church notes that in Eucharists devised by students the Service of the Word, heavily political and contemporary in focus, strongly overshadows the Liturgy of the Eucharist, which is added almost as a compulsory afterthought.[12])

The more the Eucharist is secularized to make it relevant, the more it is robbed of its meaning and the less likely it is to endure, except as a residual tie with tradition for persons who are reluctant to make themselves completely post-Christian. At youth Masses of the underground church, for example, the *Gloria* is omitted because "it is alien to an American way of speaking." The same is true of the Creed, although somewhat less so. An unofficial Canon is used which, consciously or otherwise, reflects an Arian viewpoint; Jesus is referred to simply as "our brother" and as having been "raised up" to be God's "first-born son." Suggested readings are from Camus, Sartre, and other modern masters, as well as a clearly unitarian passage from Emerson.[13] An Anglican All Saints' liturgy at a Canadian university commemorates "all the great persons of the past who have enriched the lives of men through their gifts of imagination and insight." [14]

At a pre-Christmas "Mass" celebrated under vaguely Roman Catholic auspices, a woman begins the service by denouncing a print of a Raphael Madonna and Child on the wall, because of its "coldness" and "separatism." Christmas, she says, means "getting out of the womb." The first reading is from Henry Miller's *Tropic of Capricorn* recounting that the narrator had been born a half hour after Christmas ended and suggesting that he would have been better off if his mother had broken her neck on Christmas Day. The congregation laughs uneasily, and the celebrant says, "Whew!" The creator of the rite replies, "Don't fuss, Dick, we have a light touch from *The Village Voice.*" The second reading concerns a pseudo-womb created by a New York artist, which can be purchased for six hundred dollars. During this reading the celebrant absentmindedly nibbles crumbs from the eucharistic bread, having earlier lighted a small cigar. A young man asks angrily what it means to go home for Christmas. "Usually it means just crawling back into the same old womb. With parents who don't understand us, who make a big commercial fuss over Christmas." An official Advent Collect is recited, and afterward the group partakes of the Eucharist proper. When it is over a girl says to a neighboring young man, "I guess this is about as modern as liturgy gets." "Mercy, no," he replies, "I've seen equally advanced ones in Holland, Germany, even France." [15]

When the search for a truly modern liturgy was at its height, the theologian Charles Davis, a former Roman Catholic priest, suggested that it was in fact doomed to fruitlessness, since "there is no modern form of worship, because worship itself is outmoded in the modern world and Christian faith a state of deviancy from contemporary culture." Further, he warned that radical attempts at modernization are likely to lead to "pastiche" and added that "Creative power is lacking, and the danger is that the outcome of ambitious efforts will be the disintegration, not the renewal, of traditional liturgies." Professor Davis posed a necessary choice between "the ghetto and the desert"—the former a self-consciously alien and in certain ways "pre-modern" religious community, the latter a stoical acceptance of modern secularism with all its religious dryness. He himself opted for the latter, but he saw the former as a viable choice and pointed out that no true liturgy is possible without a unified community from which it emanates.[16] The prophetic character of his words by now seems almost undeniable.

At the same time, however, the liturgical reformers' conception of "modern man" has been as much at the root of their problems as their lack of regard for tradition. Besides overemphasizing the secular character of contemporary society, ardent Christian modernizers have tended to define modern man as a faceless abstraction in contrast to the equally faceless abstraction of the church member. Numerous theologians, preachers, and liturgists exhort Christians to get out of their ghettos, become part of "the world," stop looking inward, and cease engaging in "escapist" religious activity. Yet in simple truth there is no "world" to which all men belong, except in the most generalized sense. Modern man, like all the men before him, belongs, either by choice or by birth, to numerous ghettos—family, nation, city, neighborhood, social class, occupation, recreational club, political party, *ad infinitum*. The world is not a monolithic and unified reality in the shadow of which the Church huddles off to one side; it is a collection of overlapping and interlocking "ghettos," and to the degree that the Church overlooks this fact and seeks to make itself relevant to a generalized "humanity" it loses power, character, and identity and begins to speak in exceedingly hollow-sounding tones.

The radicalization of liturgy has in fact accompanied a general sharpening of Christian awareness of social injustice; many of those who have sought to make liturgy relevant have been equally concerned to help those in need. There is, however, no necessary connection between the two attitudes, and no convincing evidence that a radicalized liturgy creates a social conscience. More commonly it has been the same restlessness and disaffection with traditional institutions which has stimulated both social activism and liturgical radicalism in the same people.

Even in its classic phase the Liturgical Movement probably embodied a higher degree of social conscience than was to be found in the Church (or secular society) at large; its leaders were always at pains to insist that liturgy has social dimensions and cannot be an end in itself. In the Church of England some of the earliest "ritualists," in Victorian times, were slum priests, and that honorable tradition has continued to the present time. Perhaps the most renowned Christian of recent years with respect to dedication to the poor, Mother Teresa of Calcutta, espouses a quite sacral and intense devotion to the Mass. Once when given a sum of money she surprised the donor by using it to buy sacred vessels for her convent chapel and told him that thereby "you will be daily on the altar close to the Body of Christ." [17]

Sacred ritual has sometimes been an escapist activity for certain devout people, although it is worth inquiring what their lives would be like if this form of escape were not available to them. However, there is virtually no human activity which cannot be used for escapist purposes if the individual is primarily bent on escape. Radical liturgists demonstrated their own worldly naïveté in not seeing that the activities in the "real world" toward which they urged Christians—election campaigns, picketing, volunteer social work, encounter groups, the study of the social sciences—are often just as "irrelevant" and "escapist" as the Latin Mass. Some of the priests who left the sanctuary for the social-welfare bureaucracies or the universities during the euphoric days of the Great Society have perhaps by now begun to wonder if their new roles are truly more meaningful than the old.

Radical liturgical communities have often sought to model themselves on the style of the early Church, which is assumed to have been simple and relatively unstructured. What they have failed to realize is that to a great extent the ethos of these modern groups is, if anything, the precise opposite of the ethos of the early Church. For the pre-Constantinian Church was nothing if it was not a sect. The unbaptized were rigidly excluded from the services. Its members had a strong sense of their uniqueness and, ultimately, their superiority over the surrounding pagan society. If ever that awareness should dull, the threat of martyrdom was present to reawaken it. The notion that the Eucharist was the means whereby they celebrated their unity with the whole world, or that their own rites were in some sense equivalent to the rites of the pagans, would have been incomprehensible to them. The temptation of the early Christians was perhaps to excessive sectarianism. The temptation of the modern underground, while in one sense sectarian, is in another sense the opposite—toward indiscriminate syncretism and a blurring of the meaning of what it is to be a Christian. Periodically it becomes necessary to restate the obvious, as the Episcopal theologian Robert Terwilliger did when he remarked:

The current jargon has it that the Eucharist is the "celebration of life." The Eucharist is not "the celebration of life" unless it is the celebration of the life of Christ. . . . This life is not the same old life of the human community as it is celebrated in ordinary or festive common meals of the family of man. . . . Strangely, this seems to be all it means now to many Christians, even those who speak knowingly of the Liturgical Movement, even those who make Eucharist in the Roman Church. . . .[18]

It is worth noting that, even as a "celebration of life," the new Eucharists can sometimes take odd forms; liturgy held when the radical priest Philip Berrigan was released from prison included a reading from the work of George Jackson, an apostle of violent revolution. (Relating the incident, a participant remarked, "Some of the career pacifists really winced at the last."[19]) One of the inestimable advantages of a stable, official liturgy is that it cannot be perverted, in its very text and rite, to partisan usage or to usages which participants may later come to regret.

Mircea Eliade observed that, although modern man conceives himself as taking responsibility for the world in a way his more religious ancestors did not, in fact his responsibility is more limited—he is content with a generally political or technological responsibility rather than a cosmic responsibility. He no longer perceives the universe as a cosmos, a living and articulated unity. Instead, it is the sum of its material parts.[20] Religion and religious ritual thus perform their greatest service for man when they seek to awaken him to this larger dimension of existence, when they persuade him to see beyond (and, most important, to wish to see beyond) the limited horizons of technological society.

Although the cult of relevance proclaims above all its desire to "serve man," there is surely no service involved in conniving with a complacent secularism and a narrow humanism. If there is an eternal dimension of reality, religion does man a priceless service in making him aware of it. Insofar as the priest, like the scientist or the politician, expresses his lack of concern for eternity, he is basically false to his calling, and he prepares the way directly for the flourishing of all those pseudo-religions which sprang up in such abundance amid the ruins of the humanist dreams of the 1960s.

Paradoxically, therefore, the most relevant liturgy is often that which is least relevant in worldly eyes. The rite of Benediction of the Blessed Sacrament, for example, was introduced in part to counter denials of Christ's Real Presence, and the disuse into which it has fallen is obviously related to a renewed skepticism about the same doctrine. As John Macquarrie has said:

. . . the importance of eucharistic worship was never greater than it is today, when the whole fabric of the Christian faith is threatened. Those who work to ensure that the holy eucharist shall be the main occasion of Christian worship, those who teach due reverence in the preparing and receiving of the sacrament, those who seek to have the blessed sacrament reserved as a focus of devotion in every church . . . are not only following in the age-old tradition of Christian devotion but are witnessing and responding to the needs of today, affirming in our world the reality of God, the one source of faith, hope, and love.[21]

The anthropologist Victor Turner has argued that sacred rituals serve man and society not as reflections or expressions of the established structure of "reality" but as events outside the texture of the ordinary. Sacred time and sacred space provide occasions when man is stripped of his normal attributes and leveled before the transcendental. Sacred rites thus make man aware of powers which are antithetical to those that maintain the normal structures of the world. Professor Turner believes that much liturgical reform has been fundamentally misconceived, in that it seeks to make ritual more conformable to contemporary social structure rather than alien to it.[22] (This is true not only of liturgies which might celebrate "bourgeois" or "establishment" values but also of "radical" liturgies which share the same underlying materialistic and naturalistic assumptions.) "Relevant" liturgies tend continuously to blend with life itself and thus become pointless; the radical disjunction of liturgy and ordinary existence is not sufficiently recognized.

Clifford Geertz, an anthropologist, has summarized the function of liturgy:

Having ritually "leaped" . . . into the framework of meaning which religious conceptions define and, the ritual ended, returned again to the commonsense world, a man is—unless, as sometimes happens, the experience fails to register—changed. And, as he is changed, so also is the commonsense world, for it is now seen as but the partial form of a wider reality which corrects and completes it.[23]

In the search to rediscover the roots of the sacred, the first two principles have perhaps now emerged:

Religious ritual which seeks consciously to become humanly relevant will in time suffer the opposite fate, while the most truly relevant ritual is that which does not relate

to man's most immediate concern but, instead, to less accessible realities which are of greater ultimate significance.
Liturgy to a great degree seeks to take the worshiper outside the normal secular world.

NOTES

1. Jean-Paul Audet, O.P., "The Future of the Liturgy," *Worship*, XLIII, 8 (October, 1969), pp. 449–64.
2. Herman Schmidt, S.J., John Tinsley, Juan Llopis, in *Liturgy in Transition*, ed. Schmidt (*Concilium*, LXII [1971]), pp. 14–29, 70–77, 121–30.
3. See, for example, Donald P. Gray, "Sacramental Consciousness-Raising," *Worship*, XLVI, 3 (March, 1972), pp. 130–40.
4. Mannion, "The Making of a Dissident," *Commonweal*, January 19, 1973, p. 346.
5. Reported by Michael Novak in *The Saturday Evening Post*, December 28, 1968, p. 67.
6. Reported by Robert Craft in *The New York Review of Books*, August 9, 1973, p. 18.
7. *Commentary*, October, 1971, p. 114.
8. Quoted in *The Times Literary Supplement*, November 13, 1970, p. 1313.
9. Joseph T. Nolan, "New Life from the Mass," *Christian Hope in the Modern World* (The Liturgical Conference, 1963), pp. 51–53.
10. Nolan, "Celebrating at Home," *The National Catholic Reporter*, March 16, 1973, p. 9; "Sacrifice: a Word Problem," *ibid.*, February 16, 1973, p. 16; "A Proposal to Put Arts in Celebration," *ibid.*, July 6, 1973, p. 9.
11. Rolland L. Stair, C.S.C., quoted in *The National Catholic Reporter*, August 17, 1973, p. 2.
12. Evert de Jong, "Liturgical Developments in Holland," *Liturgy in Transition*, p. 144.
13. Stephen W. McNierney (ed.), *The Underground Mass Book* (Baltimore, 1968), pp. 17, 24, 65.
14. Quoted by Daniel B. Stevick, *Language in Worship: Reflections on a Crisis* (New York, 1970), p. 8.
15. Emmaus House, New York City. Described by Francine du Plessix Gray, *Divine Disobedience: Profiles in Catholic Radicalism* (New York, 1970), pp. 4–10.

16. "Ghetto or Desert: Liturgy in a Cultural Dilemma," *Worship and Secularization,* ed. Wiebe Vos (Bussum, Holland, 1970), pp. 10–27.

17. See Malcolm Muggeridge, *Something Beautiful for God: Mother Teresa of Calcutta* (New York, 1971), especially p. 36.

18. "Eucharistic Preaching," *Towards a Living Liturgy,* ed. Donald Garfield (New York, 1969), p. 27.

19. Reported by Richard H. Miller, *Commonweal,* January 19, 1973, p. 343.

20. *The Sacred and the Profane,* trans. Willard R. Trask (New York, 1959), pp. 93–94.

21. "Subjectivity and Objectivity in Theology and Worship," *Worship,* XLI, 3 (March, 1967), p. 160.

22. "Passages, Margins, and Poverty: Religious Symbols of Community," *Worship,* XLVI, 7 (September, 1972), pp. 390–412; 8 (October, 1972), pp. 482–94.

23. "Religion as a Cultural System," *The Religious Situation: 1968,* ed. Donald R. Cutler (Boston, 1968), p. 680.

CHAPTER 3

The Cult of Spontaneity

The first insoluble contradiction in the attempt to reform liturgy radically was the impossibility of transforming a "vertical" rite into something "horizontal" without destroying it in the process. The second was the equal impossibility of metamorphosing an essentially formal rite into something spontaneous.

In the classic period of the Liturgical Movement, just before the Second Vatican Council, the monk and spiritual writer Thomas Merton had warned against zealotry among liturgical reformers and then added that even worse were the "pseudo-personalists."

Secular personalism is a kind of craze for individuality, a rage for self-manifestation in which the highest value is the *recognition* of one's own uniqueness. But the great paradox of Christian personalism is this: that it consists in something else than bringing to light the unique and irreplaceable element in the faithful Christian. On the contrary, Christian personalism does not require that the inmost secret of our being become manifest or public at all. We do not even have to see it clearly ourselves.

But what is manifested, proclaimed, celebrated, and consummated in the liturgy is not my personality or your personality: it is the personality of Christ the Lord. . . .

But let us above all remember and admire the discretion, the sobriety, and the modesty with which the liturgy protects this personal witness of each individual Christian. . . .

Our spiritual modesty is protected by the reserve, the universality, and in some sense the "impersonality" of the liturgical action.

. . . We sing alike, we pray alike, we adopt the same attitudes. Yet oddly this "sameness" does not wound our individuality. . . . On the contrary it is a providential guarantee of a chaste, spiritual enthusiasm which is all the more pure because it does not have to display itself, or even be aware of itself at all.[1]

In the wake of the liturgical changes, however, "the discretion, the sobriety, and the modesty" of the official liturgy became precisely that which most distressed many reformers, and "reserve, . . . universality, and . . . impersonality" became terms of condemnation. This shift in attitude corresponded to a double use of the concept of relevance— simultaneously a turning outward toward objective social conditions and a turning inward toward subjective personal experience. A relevant liturgy might be one which spoke powerfully of social injustice, in which the aim was to bring the participant to a state of self-forgetfulness sufficient to elicit genuine sacrifices for the sake of others. It might also be an even stronger concentration on self, almost to the point of forgetfulness of the existence of others. When disaffected worshipers said, "The Mass doesn't do anything for me," liturgists no longer responded, as they once had, by insisting that the Mass is a deep mystery into whose spirit the individual must seek to penetrate by prayer, study, patience, and humility. They, rather, acknowledged that the Mass would indeed have to be changed to make it capable of speaking to a wide audience. A crucial shift of the profoundest importance was thus negotiated, but its seriousness was little noted at the time.

The implications were soon enough clear, however. Worshipers would no longer approach the rites with reverence and deference, seeking to be educated to the proper comprehension. Rather, the subjective state of the individual was itself taken as normative, and it came to be widely held that the Church has an obligation to adapt worship to that subjectivity. Necessarily, therefore, the transcendental character of liturgy—its task of lifting man above himself—was dangerously obscured, and ritual was increasingly put in the service of human needs and desires, not an altogether illegitimate function but one which had in the past been kept carefully subordinated to the greater function. Given the radical uniqueness and instability of each person's subjectivity, it was also made inevitable that liturgy itself could not be fixed to any significant degree but would be subject to constant experimentation. Predictably, some worshipers tried numerous new approaches to liturgy without coming upon the one uniquely suited to their needs, and concluded that liturgy was a dead end.

The extreme positions articulated by a few of the zealots —the Mass as a good cocktail party, or the skaters at Rockefeller Center as celebrants of authentic liturgy—were in fact not so extreme given the new assumptions which many liturgists adopted. If liturgy is to celebrate life, then whatever is truly celebratory can be seen as true liturgy. A Mass performed without a spirit of celebration is inauthentic, while a party which is joyful and recreational becomes a sacrament. Not all liturgical reformers accepted these conclusions, but the more radical pursued them to their logical outcome.

The anomaly has come to be present even among persons who did not join the underground church and who continue worshiping according to the prescribed rituals. Two elements in the reformed liturgy seem to lend themselves to the "horizontal" and to the spontaneous—the petitions and the exchange of peace. In the first, members of the congregation can, if they wish and if the group is small enough, express what is closest to their hearts, in language which comes naturally. In the second, advanced liturgical thought has come to urge that the exchange of peace not be a formal and restrained gesture like a handshake but a warm and spontaneous expression of affection—prolonged embraces, kisses, moving about the group to greet as many people as possible. The difficulty is in the fact that, for those who seek in the Mass some means of expressing personal individuality and personal concerns, the petitions and the exchange of peace become in fact the centers of the ritual, those points at which feelings can be articulated, at which the worshiper is not restricted to a formal and prescribed service. By contrast the readings, the Offertory, the Consecration, and the Communion come to have a secondary place. It seems obvious that, for people of this persuasion, the exchange of peace is usually the high point of the service, almost in fact that which makes the service meaningful. It can scarcely be otherwise if what one expects in the Eucharist is primarily the celebration of a warm sense of community.

Before the Council, H. A. Reinhold, stating what most liturgists would probably then have accepted as axiomatic, anticipated Thomas Merton in praising the official liturgy for saving worshipers from "the embarrassing sight of unrestrained and naked emotion," adding that "nothing is more opposed to good liturgy than histrionics and artificial display." A little later he warned of the danger of "a romantically conceived 'evangelical simplicity,' formless individualism, or the victimizing of the congregation by a tasteless and uninspired mystagogue." [2]

At the time his warnings perhaps seemed unnecessary, since liturgists were generally concerned with making services more solemn and restrained, not less. The speed with which the need for spontaneity was acknowledged, however, made his words prophetic indeed, and also unheeded. Soon the desire to accommodate feelings in worship was leading to innumerable experimental liturgies in which the participants tried principally, in a variety of ways, to plumb their own depths and those of their companions. Inevitably for some, the encounter groups which came to prominence in the later 1960s proved to be the ultimate sacraments, toward which everything else had been dimly pointing.

For those who believed that organized liturgy was still a valid form of expression, however, there was no shortage of Father Reinhold's "tasteless and uninspired mystagogues" to offer their services. A Jesuit seminarian expatiated on how dull the liturgy is compared with an Alka-Seltzer advertisement. To remedy this, and to make worship truly contemporary, he proposed rites which would reflect modern life in being "too much" and "at random" but at the same time "more powerful than a slice of daily life," in fact "overwhelming." The sights and sounds of daily life would, in his proposed liturgy, "scream out for the attention they deserve." Voices and music would be loud and abrupt. Startling images would be projected on the wall, so compelling that "passivity is impossible." The creator of the service, called now a "visual rhetorician," aims to bring the participants into "violent confrontation" with their environment, which dictates that "shock, then, is a necessary element." Several films are projected simultaneously, including one on surfing, which expresses "the exuberance of humanity in the Christmas season." Christmas music is played on the loudspeakers, but vying with it are "noisy commercials for useless products and weather reports." Ideally "the congregation must be surrounded by sound, as though assaulted on all sides by noise," since this is the true contemporary experience of Christmas. For Ash Wednesday the theme of discipline could be expressed by showing films on Olympic diving or running.[3]

A German priest-liturgist described a visit to a Protestant church in Greenwich Village:

On entering, you were kissed by a coloured girl, forced up some stairs where you had to eat some unidentifiable kind of soup, and then put on trial under brilliant searchlights. You were chased through a jungle of polystyrene foam and corrugated paper, put up against a wall and photographed with arms outspread, inter-rogated, led on to the dance-floor by a girl who turned out to be a man, and finally asked by a doctor to put out your tongue, only to be given the verdict of imminent death. . . .

The priest then added defiantly, "Why shouldn't a church be the place in which we are confronted with everything which is beautiful and repressive, intelligible and inconceiv-able in our lives? Or is a church an island to retreat to from life's problems?" He thought there was little celebration in the churches because of a lack of understanding of "how modern man celebrates." [4]

Robert Terwilliger related a famous incident which con-sisted in

Harvey Cox clad in Eastern Orthodox vestments, celebrating something or other with bread, wine, incense, and so forth, at three or four o'clock on Orthodox Easter . . . in a nightclub in Boston. The celebration included multimedia presentations, music from the movie Z, the Hallelujah Chorus, and spontaneous danc-ing. The congregation . . . ran out at dawn to greet the sun. A Boston policeman, present to enforce the local law against danc-ing on Sundays, is quoted as saying, "This is not religion; it is god-damn chaos."

Father Terwilliger then added:

People may seek the Church yet once again for relief, and the relief we may give them may be a great put-on with bread and wine, incense, and balloons, even the warmth of human touching. It may be fantasy. It is not Eucharist: resurrected Christ-centered newness of life.[5]

Moderate liturgical innovators were doubtless embarrassed by the nearly mindless experiments of some of those on the fringe of the movement (although the fringe had come by 1969 to include the leadership of the Liturgical Conference). But the restating of the obvious by men like Father Terwilliger would not have been necessary if even moderates had not incautiously succumbed to a vague notion of liturgy as simply "celebration," and if they had not fallen in so easily with the fallacy that worship is supposed to be the expression of spontaneous personal feelings. The nadir of Christian spirituality in the past decade was reached when it was discovered that liturgy could fit in so readily with that ultimate expression of general spiritual bankruptcy, the Happening—the search for formless, pointless experience, the pursuit of stimulation for its own sake.

Among the many paradoxes of liturgical reform is the fact that, even among moderates who eschew the radical extremes, the attempt to make worship more personal, warm, and expressive of love has often had the opposite effect. Experimental groups sometimes broke up as deep antagonism and unbridgeable differences began to develop. Most ironically, what was intended as the ultimate gesture of love and peace became in many parishes itself a cause of dissension. Some worshipers resisted the gesture and felt it was imposed upon them. In many places this concession to the spirit of spontaneity was adopted only in obedience to the law.

The simple explanation—that a reluctance to exchange the sign of peace signifies a lack of Christian love in the congregation—is not adequate. People decline to exchange the peace not only with persons they dislike, or who are strangers to them, but also with close friends and members of their own families with whom they are on loving terms. What appears to motivate the reluctance in many cases is a sound perception of the incongruity of introducing a spontaneous gesture into a formal rite. It often appears to be an interruption of the service, and the incongruity worsens if some participants choose to make the gesture prolonged and demonstrative. The atmosphere of the liturgy allows the acceptance of formal or stylized acts, but the insertion of an act which purports to be spontaneous seems to invite skepticism and coolness. The formal handshake is accepted as a conventional sign of good will and mutual regard. To make more of it is to tread on very personal territory which may turn out to be guarded, and for good reason. The cult of spontaneity throughout American culture suggests that shallow, insincere, effervescent emotions can be summoned up on short notice and at little personal cost. As this phenomenon appears in the liturgy it often provokes feelings of caution, reserve, and suspicion rather than their opposites.

Major attempts to create liturgical Happenings, as well as small gestures like the sign of peace, also reveal an unforeseen paradox: nothing becomes so contrived as that which must be continuously spontaneous. Many liturgical reformers have expressed admiration for the Quaker use of silence in worship, but without perceiving that one of the reasons for those long silences is the recognition that much of the time the worshipers will not have anything that is worth saying. Truly spontaneous and creative moments in liturgy are rare, and the desire to make them a regular feature of worship is likely to lead to what is in reality stale, uninspired, and manipulative.

The desire for spontaneity in worship is also directly related to the tendency to make it relevant by evacuating much of its religious content. If the Mass is ultimately a deep supernatural mystery, then no human feelings and perceptions will ever be adequate to express its meaning. As a divine mystery it lies not only beyond intellectual comprehension but also beyond suitable emotional response. Thus so long as human perceptions and experiences are regarded as somehow central to the rite (they do have a legitimate, carefully subordinated place), it is short-circuited into merely natural channels and ceases to possess a divine character. Whatever it may thereby gain in immediacy it loses in richness, depth, and complexity.

Clifford Geertz theorizes that religious rituals aim to stimulate and preserve both "moods and motivations" of behavior, in accordance with a general view of the universe embodied in religious symbols. Of the two, moods are more evanescent and unreliable, while motivations are deeper and more enduring and do not necessarily have to do with feelings.[6] Liturgical experimentation in the past decade seems to have concentrated for the most part on the evocation of moods, which is inevitable when relevance is defined very narrowly to apply to the present concrete situation in a particular group. This has led to a remarkable degree of instability, internal conflict, and eventually even disintegration within many groups and to a liturgy which becomes less and less meaningful the more it is changed. There has been little concern for the deeper and more abiding human elements in worship, the ingrained and habitual attitudes which have grown out of it over long years and which have often been cavalierly dissipated amid thoughtless change.

The anthropologist A. R. Radcliffe-Brown defined ritual as involving a "symbolic statement of sentiments necessary for social life,"[7] and if the term "social life" is understood broadly enough this definition is applicable to religious ritual as well, since the total social life of the believer necessarily involves the divine reality, insofar as it impinges on human life. The importance of the definition is in the affirmation that ritual is a "symbolic" statement of these sentiments, not necessarily a realistic one. The confusion of these two realms, as much as anything, has wreaked havoc with much liturgical reform.

A spontaneous liturgy will of necessity be a liturgy which impoverishes itself because it will have to be based on whatever sentiments are available at the time of celebration. On rare occasions it may be a profound religious experience, although the likelihood of a whole group of worshipers all having mystical experiences simultaneously is not very great. Not only will the liturgy be dead when its creators are tired or jaded, not only will it fail to proclaim the Redemption if the creators are suffering fear or disappointment, but it will inevitably latch onto whatever emotions—trivial or sublime, creative or destructive, Christian or pagan—can stimulate it and provide it with a focus. By definition, therefore, it becomes a liturgy which cannot be transcendent, which cannot help the worshipers to rise above themselves, which keeps falling into narcissism. Robert Terwilliger has even questioned the validity of the "dialogue homily," since, as he points out, the preacher is supposed to preach in the name of Jesus, yet Jesus preached authoritatively, not giving all sides of the question and not exchanging ideas in a democratic fashion.[8] It is not an exaggeration to say that many experimental liturgies have amounted primarily to a sharing of confusions, which is never what Christian worship has been supposed to be, in any church whatever.

By now several further principles of sacred worship have begun to delineate themselves:

In Catholic ritual the participants seek to articulate not primarily their immediate subjective sentiments but what might be called their "true selves"—the habitual, ingrained attitudes of faith which endure through doubts and crises, the highest expressions of worship toward which the individual aspires.

*Within Catholicism, subjective and spontaneous personal
devotion has been given play primarily in nonliturgical worship, which the Church has approved while also insisting on
the primacy of liturgical worship which is impersonal and
objective.*

It may be possible to insert occasional spontaneous gestures into the official liturgy—applause, heartfelt "Amen,
brothers!" or hats tossed into the air[9]—but it can be done
only sparingly and will often have the mark of incongruity,
since the entire tone of the liturgy implies that the worshiper
should transform himself to enter into the spirit of the rite,
not use the rite as a vehicle for personal expression. To omit
parts of the Mass casually because they "do not speak to"
the participants, or to add alien elements which seem to be
relevant, is to miss the point that liturgy, as the official
prayer of the Church, expresses the total beliefs and symbolic attitudes of that Church. Insofar as the official liturgy
becomes the raw material for experimentation, for adaptation to the needs of particular groups, it is transformed radically into something it was never meant to be and soon
begins to lose its power, its meaning, even its coherence. A
common liturgy presupposes a common faith and a common
life of grace. To the extent that a participant in liturgy finds
less or even offensive, the honest course is to depart the
Church.

For the worshiper who remains within the Church it is
important that unrealistic and unnecessary expectations not
be built up, a tendency of which the Liturgical Movement
was sometimes guilty even in its classic period. It matters
little whether the worshiper feels contrition during the *Confiteor* or the Prayer of Humble Access, is carried away with
joy during the *Gloria,* experiences a perceptible quickening
of faith during the Creed, or a deep sense of the divine in-
dwelling after Communion. The level of true faith, as all

competent theologians have always recognized, lies beneath such sentiments, as a habitual and ingrained commitment of the entire person, a locus of reality more authentic than those layers of personality which are prone to sudden and spectacular eruption. A very "creative" celebrant or a preacher who gives highly "personal" homilies is ultimately reduced to offering the congregation his own finite and flawed personality. One of the greatest advantages of an established worship and a preaching which bases itself on the beliefs of the whole Church is that it enables even the poorest of priests to give his people something more.

NOTES

1. "Liturgy and Spiritual Personalism," *Worship*, XXXIV, 9 (October, 1960), pp. 503–5.
2. *The American Parish and the Roman Liturgy* (New York, 1958), p. 15; *Bringing the Mass to the People* (Baltimore, 1960), p. 37.
3. Richard A. Blake, S.J., "Visual Rhetoric for the Word of God," *Worship*, XLII, 5 (May, 1968), pp. 292–98.
4. Günter Rombold, "Creative Freedom in the Parish Church," *Liturgy in Transition*, ed. H. Schmidt (*Concilium*, XLII [1971]), pp. 82, 84.
5. "Eucharistic Preaching," *Towards a Living Liturgy*, ed. Donald Garfield (New York, 1969), pp. 27–28. For Harvey Cox's account of the same event see *The Seduction of the Spirit* (New York, 1973), pp. 156–65.
6. "Religion as a Cultural System," *The Religious Situation: 1968*, ed. Donald R. Cutler (Boston, 1968), pp. 643, 649–50.
7. *Structure and Function in Primitive Society* (Glencoe, Ill., 1952), p. 157.
8. "Eucharistic Preaching," p. 31.
9. These are the suggestions of Joseph T. Nolan, "Spontaneity in Worship," *The National Catholic Reporter*, May 11, 1973, p. 14.

CHAPTER 4

The Loss of History

If the reform of the liturgy led to the discovery by many reformers that the sense of the sacred was an obstacle to good worship rather than its precondition, it also stimulated the awareness that authentically renewed worship did not involve a recovery of lost or distorted traditions, as had been thought, but rather, the abandonment of most traditions in favor of a bold striking out into uncharted contemporary territory. Within a few years of the Second Vatican Council, staff members of the Liturgical Conference were quoting with approval a jazz musician's complaint:

. . . what good does it do for a minister to show a good film and speak about the relevance of the Church in our daily life if we are going to follow the sermon with a hymn from another century? Right away we have effectively reminded the congregation that we are protected and separated from the world.[1]

There were other expressions of the same sentiment,[2] and numerous experimental groups tried to apply it.

The mood which followed the conservative reforms of the Council was one of swelling exuberance at the sense of emancipation from the hand of tradition, the dead weight of the past. It was a mood which would be quickly dissipated, leaving a good deal of bitterness and confusion, by the discovery that the Council had not issued a charter for endless liturgical experimentation, and the practically simultaneous discovery that even most of the unauthorized experiments were not proving highly satisfying. Liturgical experimenters found themselves caught between the remnants of a past they were eager to be rid of and a future which somehow refused to be born.

There were, as already indicated, invalid generalizations about "modern man." Among other things the most radical innovators failed to notice that few contemporary men choose to live only amid the artifacts of their own time. Well-made old houses are if anything more popular than newer ones. The antique market provides steady opportunities for decoration and investment. Proposals to destroy historic landmarks raise public outcries. Museums are crowded by people wanting to see old masters, and symphony orchestras have trouble filling their seats if they play mostly modern works. For better or for worse, a determined holding onto a good deal of the past seems to be a feature of modern man, probably because he senses how fragile these survivals really are.

A flourishing and healthy culture is one which demonstrates creative power but also finds ways to make the best of the past a living part of the present. Either petrifaction or frenetic innovation is a sign of cultural pathology. The Second Vatican Council attempted to eliminate the former danger, only to see its actions interpreted as a justification for the latter. In liturgy as in other things there was a symbolic slaying of the fathers, followed by a joyful shout of "All things are now permitted."

Unlimited private experimentation was initially justified as an attempt to translate the essential meaning of the old rites into idioms more accessible to modern man. There was talk about altering the forms of worship or theology without altering their essential content, but that was a naïve or disingenuous ambition from the beginning. The Episcopalian liturgist Daniel Stevick later pointed out that a crisis of style always masks a crisis of identity.[3] If people suddenly began to find that the Latin of the Mass, or the English of the Book of Common Prayer, or numerous traditional rites, no longer spoke to them adequately, this indicated not simply a need for that modern panacea—"better communication"—but a desire to rethink radically the very foundations of belief and worship. The reformers who set out to simplify, clarify, and cleanse traditional worship soon found themselves being drawn toward the creation of new forms which expressed radically redefined beliefs: the Eucharist as celebration of community or of human life, worship as a way of promoting ethical sensitivity or providing emotional experiences for the participants.

A circular action was involved, which soon became a vicious circle leading to the rapid breakdown of liturgy. Liturgical innovators were vaguely dissatisfied with the traditional forms but did not realize the extent of their dissatisfaction until they began to experiment. As they peeled away the layers of historical accretions to liturgy, they found, sometimes with shock, sometimes with satisfaction, that the core of belief which underlay traditional worship was not at all the same as their own, that what was involved in liturgical reform was nothing less than a profound revolution in the nature of belief itself. The vicious circle formed, however, because if a crisis of belief provokes a crisis of worship it is also true that a crisis of worship provokes further crises of belief. The symbols and the reality they were meant to express were so closely welded that it was impossible to alter one without altering the other.

The drive for radical liturgical innovation thus became a principal cause of the widespread crisis of faith which began to appear in the Church. In its origins this crisis affected only a relatively few persons, who were moved to begin the restless search for a truly "relevant" modern liturgy. As radically transformed liturgies began to be celebrated, however —in colleges, seminaries, high schools, convents, living rooms, sometimes even in churches—the crisis became more and more a public thing and began to affect more and more people. The stability of the liturgy for so long had been an effective public symbol of the stability and unity of belief and, equally important, it had been a means by which this stability and unity were preserved and reinforced. Now the diversity and sometimes the shocking unfamiliarity of liturgy became an equally effective public symbol of the instability and diversity of belief and a means of intensifying and propagating this. Many persons found themselves on a roller coaster going they knew not where. They had bought a ticket for the car because they wanted something new, interesting, more consciously contemporary than what they had; they had no idea that the car would never again return to the same stop, that the ride might turn out to be endless and endlessly jolting, unless at some point they simply asked to get off and walked away. The more liturgy was reformed to make the ancient faith meaningful in modern terms, the more it tended to diverge from the ancient faith. As Robert Redfield said about Indians in Yucatán, "Men cease to believe because they cease to understand, and they cease to understand because they cease to do the things that express the understandings." [4]

Whether or not radical experimentation has succeeded in forging an authentic and viable new form of Christianity, one of its first and most important effects was a massive loss of contact with the Catholic past, a fact which was often not noticed at first or was even denied, but then just as often came to be celebrated as a blessing and a liberation. There was consistent, sometimes aggrieved, talk about the meaninglessness of traditional rites, with the jettisoning of a good deal of this tradition regarded as a prerequisite to liturgical renewal.[5] (Sometimes the traditions thus dismissed were among the things which liturgists before the Council had regarded as beautiful and important.) These traditions were rejected on the grounds that they were either literally meaningless, sometimes even explained as the neurotic repetition of compulsive acts, or as expressing false meanings—too closely tied to a traditional theology of the supernatural. It is no exaggeration to say that many innovators came to hate the Church's past as largely a history of tyranny and superstition and especially came to hate the Church's immediate past, the milieu in which they themselves had been formed and which they now saw as a deformation, a perversion of real Christianity, an immense burden to be shed. There came to be a good deal of bitterness about the present state of the Church, cynicism about its past, and malicious ridicule directed even at things which had previously been considered sacred. Often these feelings surfaced in people who had earlier given few hints of such dissatisfaction, who may even have seemed like serene believers. Many who did not share these feelings nevertheless found them understandable and saw no cause to protest against them.

Some liturgical innovators plunged into secularism unknowingly because they were motivated, without realizing it until much later, by what Mircea Eliade calls profane man's desire to empty himself of the past, to create himself completely without the givens of a sacral universe.[6] The anthropologist who has written most perceptively about the contemporary religious crisis, Mary Douglas, argues that the destruction of ritual deprives men of the means by which to "articulate the depth of past time," so that it becomes psychologically necessary once again to return to the beginning to start over again.[7]

The Catholic Church has always placed great weight on

the authority of Tradition, especially in response to those religious groups which have sought to deny it. Although it can be perverted into a dead conservatism, a way of blunting legitimate prophetic criticism by claiming in effect that "whatever is, is right," fundamentally the exaltation of Tradition is the way by which the Church accepts history and accepts the linear flow of time. Thus the Church of history has never been overly troubled at the warning that many of its practices were not in use in the early Church; it accepts the movement of time and the need for organic changes of the kind which T. S. Eliot said occur slowly and often even imperceptibly.

Several further principles with regard to the sacred are now becoming evident:

The radical and deliberate alteration of ritual leads inevitably to the radical alteration of belief as well.

This radical alteration causes an immediate loss of contact with the living past of the community, which comes instead to be a deadening burden.

The desire to shed the burden of the past is incompatible with Catholicism, which accepts history as an organic development from ancient roots and expresses this acceptance in a deep respect for Tradition.

Every people has a past, and contact with this past can be kept alive in various ways—by study, by a conservative social structure, by preserving old artifacts, by referring new problems to older precedents for solution. All of these have been utilized by the Catholic Church in various ways, but none has been so important as ritual worship itself. Since liturgy is the great central activity in which all members of the Church participate, it is the uniquely effective vehicle by which the Church's historical identity is preserved. It serves this purpose in subordination to its primary purpose

as the means by which men worship God, but the act of
worship in Catholicism is not separable from an awareness
of this historical identity. This is formulated in the crucial
principle whose implications have been so widely ignored
in the midst of liturgical experimentation: *Lex orandi; lex
credendi* (loosely, As the Church prays, so also it believes).

The desire to return to the beginnings, to start over again,
periodically exercises a great appeal over men, either in communities like churches or in their individual lives. It is always, however, an admission of defeat, that history has
become so burdensome or meaningless that it has to be
abolished in favor of a myth of timelessness. Thus when
liturgical innovators said they wished to take history seriously, by advancing beyond a frozen liturgy which appeared
to absolutize one point in time (the time of St. Pius V, when
the Roman Mass was fixed in its form), they did not attend
to this other factor present in their longings which would
ensure that history was to become not more meaningful but
less. It was soon impossible to take history seriously because
so much of the past appeared meaningless and, as clear-eyed
observers soon noted, it is gratuitous and foolish to assume
that a Church which has had so bleak a history for so many
centuries can now hope for a glorious future.

The Protestant Reformers of the sixteenth century did
not, however, recreate the conditions of the early Church.
Even the radical Protestants of that time, the Anabaptists,
did not achieve that goal, and the major Protestant leaders
condemned much of the Anabaptist effort. The yearning to
begin again always proves a disappointment, and the journey
back to the sources always ends up somewhere else. Even in
its classic period there were some persons in the Liturgical
Movement who dreamed of recreating the original Christian
liturgy, and after the Council radical departures from official liturgy were sometimes justified on the grounds that
they were efforts to emulate the simplicity of the early

Christians. But such austerity soon lost its appeal, and experimentation moved toward all manner of innovations
which would have been shocking to the early Christians.
Most significant was the attitude toward Scripture. Dissatisfied Catholics often criticized the Church for being too
unbiblical, for espousing a traditionalism which could coun-
tenance radical departures from the Scripture. The Second
Vatican Council aimed to be, among other things, a reaffir-
mation of the importance of Scripture in the Church and an
erasing of any opposition between Scripture and Tradition.
This, it was hoped, would provide a salutary cleansing and
purifying of the life of the Church, through renewed contact with its roots. To some extent it did. However, soon the
ardent biblicism of avant-garde Catholics began to change,
through an increased acceptance of the "demythologizing"
of Scripture urged by the German Protestant theologian
Rudolf Bultmann. Little in the New Testament was now to
be taken as historically accurate. While an attitude of reverence was not jettisoned altogether, the attitude of scholarly detachment began to supersede it. Scripture was conceded no absolute authority, in that the insights of modern
man came to be the basis on which the continued relevance
of various passages of Scripture was judged. Finally, although the Church's list of canonical books of the Bible had
been devised originally to designate which were suitable for
reading in the divine liturgy, the Bible was increasingly
superseded in experimental liturgies by readings from other
sources. It came to have no more (though also perhaps no
less) importance than a great range of writings both religious and secular. Ironically, the Church which had been
accused of not paying enough attention to the Bible continued to read the Scripture from its lecterns each day, while
the underground church more and more proclaimed Henry
Miller or *The Village Voice*. Another principle had become
clear:

The attempt to begin over again by returning to the community's ancient sources tends to result in the discovery that the sources themselves are not fully relevant; the locus of the search then shifts to contemporary culture itself.

The attempt to change religious ritual radically was made in the name of serving man, on the assumption that the traditions of the past were a burden on modern men which needed to be lifted. The result, however, was a profound disservice to the people of the Church, because they had the effect of cutting them off from so much of their own past. Ritual, according to Mary Douglas, articulates the deepest order of the universe and expresses the community's sense of its historical continuity.[8] Thus at the cavalier destruction of so much Catholic ritual, people suddenly found themselves cut off from their pasts, driven into confusion and disorientation. They had become modern, if by modern is understood a rootless living only in the present. As Mary Douglas has said:

We arise from the purging of old rituals simpler and poorer, as was intended, ritually beggared, but with other losses. . . . Only a narrow range of historical experience is recognized as antecedent to the present state. Along with celebrating the Last Supper with the breaking of bread, or the simplicity of fishermen-apostles, there is a squeamish selection of ancestors . . . the anti-ritualists have rejected the list of saints and popes and tried to start again without the load of history.[9]

Toward the end of the iconoclastic decade of the 1960s the peculiar phenomenon of a fashionable and highly commercialized nostalgia emerged—regular revivals of the clothes and music of earlier decades (including the recently departed 1950s). The only remedy against nostalgia is to ensure that what is significant in the past remains alive in the present.

If an established ritual expresses the community's sense

of its deepest self and its deepest order, the destruction of that ritual necessarily expresses the opposite, and the symbolic message conveyed to many in the Church by the chaotic state of liturgy after the Council was precisely that the universe too is in a chaotic state, that man has no ability to free himself from the inexorable and contradictory demands of contemporary history, that he is a creature of his time and little more. If the old liturgy aimed to create a profound order, much of the new liturgy precisely tended to create disorder. Part of this was in the naked assertion that liturgy, which had long been considered sacred and thus to be tampered with only cautiously, was now considered a human invention entirely, to be manipulated for human purposes. This was supposed to assure man of his new freedom and creativity. Instead, in many cases it deprived him of his sense of belonging to a cosmic order, of his ability to reach beyond time and culture. As anthropologists like Victor Turner and Mircea Eliade have pointed out, the experience of ritual has been the experience of sacred time, or of timelessness, of time outside time.[10] Thus experimental liturgies which were intended to celebrate man's secular ability to create and mold his world often, instead, symbolized his unfree place in that world. The most avant-garde liturgies tended to become preoccupied with the evident hopelessness of so much contemporary life: escape from the womb, mysterious and frightening contrived happenings in a church, bewildering bombardment by random sights and sounds. Another principle had been clarified:

The attempt to achieve freedom by escaping from the burdens of tradition tends to result in a new enslavement to a chaotic present.

A major cause of the new sense of chaos, which produced unhappiness and disorientation in many people who had previously lived relatively serene lives within the order established by the Church, was the obvious manipulation of ancient symbols for new purposes—the bread and wine of the Eucharist as a primarily human communion, for example. Closely related was the sudden abandonment of numerous other symbols, with the clear implication that there is nothing in the liturgy so sacred that it cannot be eliminated in the quest for a contemporary idiom. One of the great early anthropologists, Bronislaw Malinowski, suggested that the reverence of primitive people for tradition is based on their awareness of how great a cost was required to gain whatever knowledge the tribe possesses, so that it should be treasured jealously.[11] In the economy of the Church, reverence for tradition has had the same root, since spiritual insights are also bought only at great cost. Both Victor Turner and Louis Bouyer, among others, have suggested that a fixed ritual serves the function of preserving deep spiritual truths through periods when they are not fully understood, until such time as they once again become meaningful.[12] The decision to jettison so much of tradition in the past decade has often been made rather lightly, with no thought for its long-term consequences or how the elements thus eliminated might be preserved for some possible future usefulness. (The liturgical revolution involved, among other things, a shift in emphasis from the liturgist as a man of deep learning and profound understanding of the Church's traditions to the liturgist as innovator in empathetic contact with modern culture.)

Many persons withdrew from active participation in the life of the Church after 1966 on the grounds that the Church was irrelevant and old-fashioned, and its traditional liturgy was often given a major share of the blame, especially for the disaffection of young people. (Although the failure of so many of these people to find experimental liturgies satisfying suggests that even more strenuous liturgical reform would not have helped them.) The relationship of cause and effect in such cases is difficult to disentangle, however. The officially mandated liturgical changes were being implemented as early as 1964 and were largely in effect before the flood of departures from the Church and from the priestly and religious life began. So long as the liturgy was stable, so was Church membership. As with other changes in the Church, the disaffection with liturgy seems to have come about not because the liturgy did not change but because it did. The sense of the meaning of tradition was broken; symbolically there had been a repudiation of the past which the fathers of the Second Vatican Council had certainly not intended but which their actions signaled to some people. Looking for guiding signs, many persons thought they were being told that the Church would now adapt itself thoroughly to contemporary culture. This seemed, then, like a new certainty, a new official policy to replace the old traditionalism. As it became clear that there were definite limits beyond which the Church refused to adapt, the signals once again became confusing. Some people felt they had been defrauded, both because they had once been taught to believe in the sacredness of traditions which turned out to be expendable and because they had then come to expect an unrestrained embrace of modernity which also proved illusory. Some priests were concerned to minister to these people by providing the advanced liturgies which might show that the Church could be modern. Such liturgies tended to have the opposite effect, however, since the new and manipulative use of the sacred symbols was merely a dramatization of the breakdown of the old order, of the final dying of traditional beliefs. This was their effect not only on many troubled and searching worshipers but also, finally, on many priests as well.

The bitterness of many of those caught in this historical trap was due in part to the inescapable dosage of self-hatred which was part of it. They had been intimately involved with the old Church. It had been their spiritual nurture and had done much to form them. At one time they had perhaps been happy and purposeful within it. Like the rejection of one's parents, it proved to be impossible to reject the old Church without also rejecting a large part of oneself. They were now cut off from spiritual traditions which had once seemed great and profound. If they had gained at least an apparent larger measure of freedom, it was in a world which was colder, more barren, more matter-of-fact than the one they had inherited. At a time when alienation has become a major concern of social analysts, it has proved a short-sighted and counter-productive strategy to encourage people in the discarding of their inherited religious identities. The ancestors of today's disillusioned American Catholics were people who experienced an even greater threat of alienation as they literally uprooted themselves to journey to a strange and often unfriendly land. In that exodus their liturgies were among the things which most effectively kept them as people able to transcend their sufferings.

Traditional liturgy helps men to free themselves from historical determination by making accessible to them modes of Christian life from other ages than their own. It proclaims that no man is bound simply by the customs of his own time, and hence its "irrelevance" is in certain ways its glory.

The religious revolution of the later 1960s aimed to be, among other things, a turning from the past (Christians were thought to be too conservative, inclined to look backward at a supposedly more religious era now gone) and a turning to the future. In that sense, if one dimension of history was being lost, another was being recovered. The eschatological aspect of Christianity was given renewed emphasis, the expectation of a transformed future world in which the will of God would at last be fulfilled. Christians were to emancipate themselves from the past, but thereby were enabled to take responsibility for the future.

An orthodox Christian notion was made to fit too easily with frenzied and euphoric fashions, however. For a brief time it was possible to think that "revolution" was occurring, whose locus was primarily on the college campuses where students organized themselves to resist government policies in every area, radical ideologies were resurrected which had been forgotten since the 1930s, and some apparently solid institutions (mainly the colleges themselves) proved to be remarkably vulnerable to pressure for change. Joined to the growing Black Power movement and the incipient Women's Liberation movement, student radicalism seemed to promise a thorough overhaul of the American political and economic system, and some Church members threw themselves into this struggle with an unabashedly religious fervor. Before long the improbability of "revolution" in any meaningful sense of the term became obvious, and the focus shifted to "cultural revolution." Once again avant-garde Christians professed to see deep religious significance in, for example, Charles Reich's *The Greening of America,* which predicted the coming transformation of society through a profound new consciousness that was being born in young people. By the early 1970s, however, college students were once again frankly interested in material security, and the counter-culture was in deeper trouble than even the Church. The future-oriented Christians of a few years before were left either in various kinds of disillusionment or with the tattered but still serviceable dogma that Christians are distinguished by their hope in the face of despair. In the meantime, however, this Christian hope had been emptied of most of its religious content.

Max Weber has pointed out that in times of rapid change, when old forms have been destroyed or weakened severely but new ones have not yet been created, the "charismatic leader" is likely to appear, who offers in his person the certainty which traditional institutions can no longer provide. He is unpredictable and uncontrollable and appears to understand the drift of history.[13] The most remarkable development of the early 1970s was the phenomenon of formerly radical, militantly political, secular, and often corrosively skeptical young people placing themselves under the implicit authority of Hindu gurus or becoming "Jesus freaks." "Modern" man's need to emancipate himself from religious domination proved to be of very short duration. In the Church itself equivalent leaders appeared, like Bishop Pike or Harvey Cox, whose personal odysseys came to be accepted as normative religious models by many disaffected Christians.

The atmosphere among radical Christians for a time closely resembled what has been described by sociologists as the "millenarian temperament," a phenomenon which may still be found in extreme Protestant sects but can exist in other guises. In the overheated atmosphere that began to cool after 1970 it had a largely secular thrust, even among Church people, and it attracted persons of considerable education and sophistication rather than the simpler people who usually join millenarian groups.

Generally stimulated by the experience of social breakdown or rapid social change, millenarianism often involves an absolute condemnation of the present as evil, and the concomitant appeal to either a mythical and distant past or an equally mythical future, which may be imminent. The kingdom of God is not thought to exist in some "otherworld" but will be established on earth itself. The millenarian has a strong sense of belonging to an elite which is preparing the way for this kingdom, in the face of opposition by a majority of ignorant and ungodly people. There is a general rebellion against authority, often a rapid turnover in the leadership of the movement itself, a compulsion to violate taboos deliberately, and a tendency to attract nonconformists to membership. Aggressive acts are sometimes justified. Although such movements can be nonpolitical, they may also link religion and politics if the latter is recognized as a possible means of achieving the millennium. The failure of the kingdom to arrive as predicted does not necessarily lead to the movement's demise but may simply require a reformulation of its message.[14]

Groups answering to this general description, and claiming a religious inspiration, have existed both inside and outside the Church in the past decade, their activities directed at either the secular state or the Church, sometimes at both. They have manifested a spirit which is not totally illegitimate from a Christian viewpoint, except where it becomes too fanatical or too secular. However, they have not manifested that clear-eyed worldiness which religious secularizers originally aimed at, and their existence suggests yet another principle:

The abandonment of religious traditions and the sense of the sacred tends to stimulate the formation of millenarian groups with intense but usually short-lived eschatological expectations. Their existence usually masks a hunger to reestablish religious certainties previously abandoned, although these may be put at the service of a largely secular gospel.

The alternative to millenarianism, of much lower emotional intensity and probably also affording considerably less satisfaction as a philosophy of life, is the modern idea of Progress, which the breakdown of sacred traditions also helps to release. Progress is a satisfying belief in that it summons the individual into a happier and more fulfilling future. It also tends to be alienating in that it requires the almost constant rejection of values and modes of living which have become familiar. The past is not regarded as a spring which constantly feeds the present, which gives depth and grounding to life, but as something which is continually outgrown, which must be continually discarded as burdensome and retarding. The self-evident superiority of the present over the past, and the equal superiority of the future over the present, are generally taken for granted.

Victor Turner believes that effective ritual must have something archaic about it, which is not the same as something irrelevant or dead, and that attempts to modernize liturgy radically are likely to have disastrous effects on it.[15] An additional principle can be formulated to express this:

Catholicism, although open to change, manifests a decided bias toward stability and toward the preservation of the past. This is because one of its principal tasks in the world is to witness to the reality of eternity; hence it cultivates what is timeless, enduring, and stable to serve as hints of eternity.

In Catholicism, it is necessary to recall once again, Tradition itself is seen as a legitimation of truth, although various individual traditions may be false. The sociologist Peter Berger has pointed out that, in a world where few ideas are credible purely on their own merit but most depend on some social support for their plausibility, the force of tradition is one of the most powerful of these, or at least has been in most societies.[16] The abandonment of tradition is not likely so much to make the individual freer as merely more susceptible to other kinds of social influence, such as the consensus of current enlightened opinion.

Catholicism seeks therefore to convey to people a sense of their participation in a great historical progression, in which the spiritual values of the past remain alive in the present in a variety of ways but especially through the Eucharist, which in traditional theology is considered as being celebrated for all believers living and dead and was often represented in earlier religious art as being celebrated in the presence of the angels and saints.

The rejection of tradition focuses the worshipers' attention on the narrow and incomplete community of present believers and shatters their sense of membership in the widest Christian community, which is the Communion of Saints.

This is reflected, among other things, in an evident decline of belief in Purgatory and of the practice of praying for the dead, even by a certain agnosticism about the afterlife. Living and dead are no longer thought to have any discernible bond. Meanwhile, Spiritualism grows as a popular movement among the sophisticated.

It has been pointed out that the struggle to preserve traditional religion always has the effect of changing it, frequently in ways which its defenders do not perceive.[17] This has been recognized by the Church in the fact that new dogmas have often been defined, and new devotions introduced, specifically in response to heresies. Orthodox definitions must always be in conformity with the original truth, but they can move the Church in directions it had not moved previously. Ironically, therefore, challenges to the Church to become relevant do usually have the effect of stimulating it to change, but not in the ways the modernizers have sought. This is one of the means by which petrification is avoided.

In Roman Catholicism a devotion to traditional liturgy almost inevitably has the effect of preserving orthodoxy, since these rituals are the concrete substance of the Church's life, in which its total meaning is embodied. In Anglicanism, however, the situation is different because of the fact that ritualism has been, since the 1850s, an insertion into Church life, an attempt to restore an earlier situation which cannot, in the nature of things, be restored with full fidelity. Although most Anglo-Catholics have probably been orthodox in their theology, Catholic liturgy has often been within Anglicanism what the "low-church" party has accused it of being: a ritual which does not sum up and symbolize the total life of the Church but in certain ways fractures that life and goes against the beliefs of many. As a decided innovation, Anglo-Catholic liturgy cannot perform unambiguously the function which Roman liturgy performs, that of conserving the traditions of the Church. Anglican ritualists have often been by temperament rebels, which can affect their theology. The phenomenon of the "high-church" modernist, like the influential English liturgist of the earlier part of this century, Percy Dearmer, is not unknown.

The relationship of ritual and tradition within Anglicanism is thus a more complicated one than it is in Roman Catholicism. The unity of the Anglican Church has been in its rites principally understood in a verbal sense—the words of the Prayer Book used by "high," "low," and "broad" churchmen, even as the visible gestures and symbols differ greatly. Thus attitudes to the language of the Prayer Book, or to traditional creedal formulations, have not divided along the same lines as attitudes toward ritual.

NOTES

1. Robert W. Hovda and Gabe Huck, "Music: We Must Learn to Celebrate," *Liturgical Arts,* XXXVIII, 2 (February, 1970), p. 43.

2. For example, see Peter Schillaci, "Celebrating Change: the Liturgy," *Worship,* XLIV, 2 (February, 1970), pp. 66–82; Helmut Hucke, "Towards a New Kind of Church Music," *Liturgy in Transition,* ed. H. Schmidt (*Concilium,* LXII [1971]), pp. 87–97.

3. *Language in Worship: Reflections on a Crisis* (New York, 1970), pp. 33–36.

4. *The Folk Culture of Yucatán* (Chicago, 1955), p. 363.

5. For example, see Benedict R. Avery, O.S.B., "A Halfway House to Aggiornamento: the Sacramentary," *Worship*, XL, 10 (December, 1966), pp. 634–49.

6. *The Sacred and the Profane*, trans. Willard R. Trask (New York, 1959), pp. 203–4.

7. *Natural Symbols* (New York, 1970), p. 20.

8. *Ibid.*, pp. 19–20, 51.

9. *Ibid.*, pp. 19–20.

10. Turner, "Passages, Margins, and Poverty," *Worship*, XLVI, 7 (September, 1972), p. 399; Eliade, *The Sacred and the Profane*, pp. 68, 85, 89.

11. *Magic, Science, and Religion* (Garden City, N.Y., 1955), p. 39.

12. Turner, "Passages, Margins, and Poverty," (cited n. 10), p. 400; Bouyer, *Liturgical Piety* (Notre Dame, Ind., 1954), p. 8.

13. *The Theory of Economic and Social Organization*, ed. Talcott Parsons (Glencoe, Ill., 1947), p. 361.

14. Yorina Talmon, "Pursuit of the Millennium: the Relation between Religious and Social Change," *Reader in Comparative Religion: an Anthropological Approach*, ed. William A. Lessa and Evon Z. Vogt (New York, 1965), pp. 526–35.

15. "Passages, Margins, and Poverty," (cited n. 10), pp. 391–92.

16. *The Sacred Canopy: Elements of a Sociological Theory of Religion* (Garden City, N.Y., 1967), p. 31.

17. David G. Mandelbaum, "Transcendental and Pragmatic Aspects of Religion," *American Anthropologist*, LXVIII, 5 (October, 1966), p. 1189.

CHAPTER 5

The Death of Community

The death of the Catholic past, as both a cause and an effect of liturgical change, was partly willed by innovators who regarded the past as a drag on the present. Virtually all these innovators were, however, convinced of the central importance of community, and it was the aim of much liturgical experimentation to heighten the sense of this community through celebration. It was the supreme failure of experimental liturgy, therefore, that it so often had the general effect of weakening and even destroying such community as already existed.

This was inevitable first of all because of the disregard of, or even hostility to, the Catholic past which many experimenters demonstrated. They set up a false opposition between a dead tradition and a living present community and thought that somehow the elimination of the former would work toward the strengthening of the latter. The conceit gained currency for a time that a community's past is somehow irrelevant to its present, although after a few years there was inevitably a renewed search for roots. Strong and vital communities are likely to be precisely those which have a significant common past of which the community is keenly aware. A community which seeks to live primarily on its past will petrify, but a community which loses contact with its past or comes to repudiate much of its past is likely to disintegrate. The past is a major factor in defining the present character of any community, and its loss tends to make the community formless and purposeless. As already suggested, the loss of the Catholic past tended among other things to obliterate people's awareness of belonging to the Communion of Saints. It can be further argued that:

The decline of a sense of tradition in the Church severely weakens not only its continuity with the ages past but also its coherence in the present age.

When liturgical radicalism was first gaining ground, a Benedictine monk proposed that "As liturgy becomes more humble, poor, and sensitive to human needs, there is every reason to believe that the Christian people will become so too. . . ." [1] It was an attractive formula, although somewhat lacking in logic. (Were the most unliturgical churches, for example the Baptists, always more morally aware?) However, it contained a truth which its formulator perhaps did not perceive: as liturgy was systematically stripped and remodeled the Catholic people became poorer not materially but spiritually; they became humbler because they were often induced to be ashamed of their Church and its past; whether they became more humanely sensitive remains uncertain.

The task of liturgical reform, as generally conceived before the Council, was to perform a series of delicate operations—the amputation of certain dead limbs, the transplantation of other parts, considerable plastic surgery—which would be successful because of the deep learning of the surgeons and their profound respect for the patient. In time, however, the learning began to seem irrelevant to many doctors, merely further evidence of a backward mentality. The respect also began to diminish, and a few surgeons even seemed to want to kill the patient; there were many who were ready to extract the living parts for use in other organisms. Altogether the delicacy and complexity of the task was underestimated even by those surgeons who had the best of intentions.

The most acute analysis of the function of religious ritual and the present liturgical crisis in the Church has been made by Mary Douglas. She points out the modern bias which has given the term "ritualist" negative connotations and suggests that the acceptance of this negative implication even by Catholic clergy is evidence of their failure to understand the nature of ritual action. For ritual is not, as both puritanism and the modern secular mind tend to insist, merely the compulsive and empty repetition of meaningless acts. Instead it represents a "heightened sensitivity to symbolic actions." Individual ritual acts function as an "economical condensation" of a whole range of symbols referring to the life of the community, and in Christianity the Eucharist is the most important of these. Mary Douglas cites Friday abstinence as another,[2] a symbol which has conveyed a diversity of meanings on a number of levels: a reminder of Christ's death, the need for asceticism on the part of Christians, the hallowing of particular days, membership in a distinct religious group, etc., etc.

Professor Douglas argues that many liturgists were insensitive to the functioning of ritual communication: "It is as if the liturgical signal boxes were manned by colour-blind signalmen." As a result:

When ritualism is openly despised the philanthropic impulse is in danger of defeating itself. For it is an illusion to suppose that there can be organization without symbolic expression. . . . Those who despise ritual, even at its most magical, are cherishing in the name of reason a very irrational concept of communication. . . .

. . . [those] who prefer unstructured intimacy in their social relations, defeat their wish for communication without words. For only a ritual structure makes possible a wordless channel of communication that is not entirely incoherent.[3]

The liturgical crisis came about originally because of a relatively small number of persons, especially certain liturgists, who found the traditional rites and symbols no longer powerful and compelling. They set about to devise new ones, or in some cases to attempt liturgies which had little dependence on symbol at all. But the circularity of the problem was soon evident. The more the symbols were discarded or altered to make liturgy relevant, the more irrelevant it became. Each alteration in the ritual conveyed the symbolic message that the ritual was indeed meaningless. Each attempt to employ old symbolism in new ways merely produced confusion and convinced still more people that the liturgy of the Church was simply incoherent. Indeed "meaningless" came to be a frequent term of dismissal applied to the liturgy, something which had rarely been done even in the days of the Latin Mass. Professor Douglas has suggested that the search for new symbols to replace the old may be fruitless because some people are simply insensitive to symbol altogether. In any case:

As soon as symbolic action is denied value in its own right, the flood-gates of confusion are opened. . . . If a people takes a symbol that originally meant something else, and energetically holds on to that subverted symbol, its meanings for their personal life must be very profound.[4]

What existed in the Catholic Church prior to the era of liturgical experimentation was a coherent and stable, even rigid, system of symbols which in turn reflected a coherent and stable, even rigid, way of life. Although the entire system might sometimes seem oppressive, it was respected and did not for the most part induce bitterness or alienation in those raised within it, because whatever else it did, it provided a focus around which human life might be structured and it provided a way by which this meaning could be expressed. The Second Vatican Council was an effort to remove the rigidities from this life without losing the coherence and stability; those who misread its intentions soon attacked the latter as well. The radicalization of liturgy perhaps occurred earlier than the same process in doctrine, the religious life, or morals, but all came to exist in symbiotic relationship: a weakening belief in the coherence of Catholic life caused a weakening attachment to the Church's liturgical symbols; but the deliberate transformation of the symbols in turn caused a further weakening of belief in the basic coherence of the Church's life.

Thus there occurred that most peculiar of all the phenomena of the postconciliar Church, the fact that as the Church became less rigid and more adaptable it drove away more and more of its members, provoked more and more rebellion, and induced more and more a sense of alienation and frustration in its people, almost as though those who were loudest in their demands for change were most angry because the changes occurred. It was soon clear, for example, that those religious orders which tried most energetically to "reform" themselves were likely to lose the most members and attract the fewest novices, that those clergy who threw themselves most eagerly into the quest for a relevant liturgy were among those most likely to leave the priesthood, and that those laymen who joined the new underground groups were among those who would soonest discover that liturgy no longer had any meaning for them, reformed or not.

All of this is explicable because extreme measures taken in the interest of change were often the last desperate efforts of people who already sensed that for them everything had lost its meaning. It is also explicable, however, because the willingness to manipulate sacred symbols in daring new ways itself destroyed whatever vestiges of meaning the symbols may still have had for these people. They often ended in a state of confusion because their own attempts to revolutionize liturgy had the direct effect of promoting confusion, and they ended in a state of bitterness because of the enormous gap between their expectations of what change would achieve and what it actually did achieve. Yet the disappointment was due at least as much to the unwittingly destructive and counter-productive policies which they had pursued as to the sluggishness of the church.

The most serious of these counter-productive policies has already been discussed—the determination to use an essentially sacral and "vertical" ritual to express an essentially humanistic and "horizontal" meaning. Whether or not such a shift in focus should have occurred, the attempt to bring it about by appropriating the liturgy for that purpose was bound to have disastrous results. From the beginning almost everyone sensed the inappropriateness of the attempt, which drove liturgical innovators to more and more extreme experiments, and which ended by destroying virtually all symbolic continuity with the historical Church. Those who became involved in such liturgies usually found in the end that Catholic life had become literally meaningless—incoherent, alien, dead, even strange. In Robert Redfield's words, they no longer believed because they no longer understood, and they no longer understood because they no longer did the things which express understanding.

The manipulation of sacred symbols to give increased meaning to the liturgy tends instead to destroy its meaning and alienate the participants from the Church's worship.

A revolutionized liturgy which sought only to put itself at the service of man failed badly even at this task because of its failure to reflect on the function of traditional liturgy in the Church. The breakup of traditional liturgy, and the other breakups in the Church which accompanied it, were a major source of anxiety and suffering to many people, not only to those extreme conservatives who went into schism rather than accept the new Mass but equally to those ardent reformers who ended by reforming themselves out of the Church. People who had lived cohesive, stable, purposeful lives of dedication often found themselves plunged into a quasi-permanent state of confusion and unhappiness. Priests especially, whose lives had been so intimately bound up with the sacred rites, found that the core of their existence tended to unravel even as the rites themselves unraveled. Although few priests before the Council had doubted that the administration of the sacraments was the principal justification for their existence, a massive crisis of clerical identity followed the liturgical changes, in which the priest's role was variously redefined as psychologist, social worker, political activist, "change agent," or even in some instances as altogether outmoded and without function.

The fragmentation and manipulation of sacred symbolism conveyed in the most dramatic and effective way possible that the community of the Church was also fragmented, probably beyond repair. For many people a uniform liturgy was itself a profoundly important symbol of a united Church, and to the extent that highly diverse liturgies were now celebrated, whether officially or unofficially, the basic sundering of Catholic unity was symbolized. The casual discarding of traditional symbols, often with the implication that there was something ridiculous or unsavory about them, symbolized effectively a Church slowly dying, piece by piece. The bold use of remaining symbols in very antitraditional ways showed quite dramatically that, whatever the Church might be in the future, it would be something far different from what it had been in the past. Those who felt uneasy over the new liturgies sensed that perhaps this future Church would have no place for them. Over it all a great pall of confusion hung: to what degree were these experiments the authentic will of the Council and the hierarchy? If not presently their will, did these changes represent the inevitable future which sooner or later the hierarchy would accept? Such symbolic conveyances were probably far more influential in establishing the tone of Catholic life in the later 1960s than any number of outright verbal assaults on traditional doctrines or hierarchical authority.

Changes which had aimed to promote community and improve dialogue ended by depriving members of the Church of the most effective means they had of communicating with one another—their sacred symbols. People became keenly aware that certain symbols acted as red flags on others within the Church (rosaries, guitars, novenas, banners, etc.), and that even symbols which were generally accepted could no longer be assumed to have common meanings for everyone, might in fact have quite divergent and opposed meanings. (The very word "celebrate" came to be one of these.) Increasingly the more avant-garde members of the Church, including some of the clergy, declined to participate in official public rituals as celebrated in the churches and moved into small groups to worship, as effective a symbol as possible in showing that the Church was now a word used to describe a radically disunited community. Liturgical change tended to promote strife rather than heal it, as some people felt it went too far and others not nearly far enough. (Ritual, which serves ordinarily as a focus of a society's unity, can under certain conditions be a cause and a symbol of dissension instead.[5]) Highly private rituals, in the sense that they were celebrated for special groups only and for the benefit of very particular tastes, tended to show that the escalating breakup of the Church would continue. This was especially the case when the private groups ceased being distinctively Catholic, and many of their members dropped out of the Church.

Liturgical radicals did not for the most part understand adequately the role of symbol and ritual in the Church. They maintained the antiritualist bias of those who tend to see it as the compulsive repetition of meaningless acts. Yet, once the rituals were tampered with, their explosive power became evident. Mary Douglas has suggested that ritual is a function of a closely knit social group, one which has a strong sense of its own identity and its own boundaries. The decline of ritual retards social organization, and the group tends to slide toward chaos and disintegration. The effectiveness of ritual depends on the people who use it having familiarity with one another, but at the same time it is the ritual which enables them to achieve this familiarity on a wide basis. Significantly for the Church, a confused and disorganized society is likely also to have a confused idea of God. Secularism, including a sense that the cosmos is dominated by impersonal forces, tends to flourish in societies which have weak boundaries and whose child-raising practices encourage a strong concentration on the self rather than on the group.[6] The sociologist Peter Berger describes rituals as reminders of deeply held values, and he believes that both the values and the rituals depend on a subculture which creates and sustains them.[7] Bronislaw Malinowski suggests that public rituals "of solemn grandeur" are necessary to place the whole weight of the community behind particular values.[8] Victor Turner points out that in effective rituals persons who may be deeply divided in other ways can meet together to sustain the cosmic order. (Thus a ritual which is too "relevant" may be ineffective because it will not transcend the divisions in the community.)[9] In the words of Clifford Geertz:

For those able to embrace them and for so long as they are able to embrace them, religious symbols provide a cosmic guarantee not only for their ability to comprehend the world, but also, comprehending it, to give a precision to their feeling, a definition to their emotions, which enables them, morosely or joyfully, grimly or cavalierly, to endure the world.[10]

As with every other aspect of Church life, liturgical change was both a cause and an effect of the fading of a sharp Catholic identity after the Council. It was an effect in that a misconceived ecumenism led many persons to suppose that a historical Catholic identity ought to be obliterated as much as possible. It was a cause in that experimentation with the liturgy tended toward merging it into broadly humanistic forms of celebration, with its distinctive symbolism either eradicated or redefined. The theology which explained this new symbolism tended then in the same direction—the sacraments as celebrations of life, for example. There was an immense loss of coherence, however, whatever may have been gained. Soon it became problematical for some people why there should be sacraments at all (or why these particular ones), why formal worship is necessary, what the value of prayer is, etc. The organizational structure of the Church was called into question by, for example, advanced priests who undertook to "preside" at the Eucharist in a nonsacral role, unvested, seated with the congregation, merely the individual conveniently designated to play the leading part. Such symbolism led inevitably to a sense of priesthood and hierarchy as somehow impositions on the people of God. The old ritual, although it had done little to promote warmth and intimacy among worshipers, had enabled quite diverse kinds of people to worship together, had allowed Catholics to worship in many parts of the world, had allowed for a communication on the symbolic level which was now becoming more and more difficult. The idea of God did indeed become confused. Most Catholics were still able to affirm a divine reality, but practically every other aspect of it (Is God personal? Can God be said properly to exist? Does God work miracles?) was called into question, and some former staunch believers drifted into agnosticism. The fact that there were no longer in the Church solemn public rituals which could command general participation seemed to signify the absence of any common identity and any commonly held values. The Church seemed to be of less and less use to people in helping them understand or endure the universe, yet the liberation from ecclesiastical domination did not on the whole seem to make people happier or freer.

Two crucial groups of persons suffered particularly in the crisis: the clergy whose entire existence was bound up with the sacred rites, and young people who began to come of age in the period of unraveling and confusion. There has been a substantial loss of young people to the Church during the period of change, and although there are many possible reasons for this, one in particular has not been adequately recognized—that younger Catholics during the past decade have had no experience of a stable and self-confident Church able to hand on its beliefs with assurance and authority. In thousands of ways what young people have perceived in the Church is a situation of seemingly boundless confusion, internal conflict, and steady disintegration. They have pronounced the liturgy and doctrines of the Church "meaningless" because they have been unable to obtain, from parents, teachers, or clergy, a coherent account of what it means to be a Catholic. The rituals which ordinarily induct the child into the community's beliefs earlier than any formal teaching have seemed confused and weak. The humanistic explanations of these rituals which have often been put forth make them seem even more confused and weak, since they offer little basis for perceiving what is unique or important about religious rituals as distinguished from innumerable secular rituals. The reluctance of young people to enter into the life of the Church has often proceeded from their apprehension that this Church may be in the process of dying and thus offers no stable, satisfying mode of life to follow. Paradoxically, it is once more the fact that the Church did change, not that it did not, which rendered it incredible in many people's eyes. The problem has been infinitely compounded by the fact that the most extreme liturgical experimentation has often been carried on in the hope of attracting the young. Such a strategy may sometimes bring short-term benefits. But in the long run it worsens the situation by impressing even deeper on young people a sense of the weakness and incoherence of Catholic life, of a symbolism which symbolizes little beyond the confused subjective state of the participants.

In the final stage of this disintegration the traditional symbols cease to be understood altogether, and there is a pointless wallowing in the liturgical backwaters. At a German "youth Mass," a juke box plays loudly in the sanctuary, while the acolytes blow cigarette smoke at the altar instead of incense. Immediately after Communion, cokes and hot-dogs are served to the participants.[11] In America a priest conducts, during Mass, a rite of divorce modeled on the Catholic marriage ceremony. The theme proclaimed is "Divided We Stand," and a soloist renders "It's Too Late, Baby." [12] In Holland a liturgy has as its principal focus a potter working under a spotlight.[13] Counterfeit liturgies are hailed as authentic, such as Leonard Bernstein's *Mass*, which employs eclectic Catholic symbolism to celebrate essentially humanistic and rather shallow ideas. There is a strong bent for syncretic ritual, in which elements are indiscriminately borrowed from various religious traditions to produce new and striking combinations. The aim is to achieve ever new and fresh experience, which is virtually the precise opposite of

the aim of genuine religious ritual. Symbolically what is proclaimed is the death of the various traditions whose symbols
are thus used, making them lawful prey for scavengers. It has
been said of some modern wedding ceremonies:

Although more marriages nowadays seem to be performed by
clergymen . . . their doctrine may not be part of anyone's daily
life or conduct. . . . The Navajo or Hopi ceremonies, the dawn
or midnight, garden or woodland nuptials, the Our Relationship
sermon by the bridal pair, all borrow sanction and dignity from
a sacramental tradition which is probably dropped as uncere-
moniously as possible after the ceremony. The couple married in
the woods do not live by the law of the woods, the Hopi vows do
not make a Hopi marriage in a modern California setting, the
girl who circles seven times around the groom or the groom who
stamps on a glass may ignore the imperatives of their actions, and
their conduct after the marriage may bear no relation to the ceremony that made it; indeed no rules of conduct for the future can
be deduced from the ceremony.[14]

A preference for eclectic ritual is not only a judgment on
the bankruptcy of the various traditions from which the rituals have been taken; it is also an implicit admission of one's
own bankruptcy, that one no longer belongs to a people who
have a distinctive way of life, a distinctive set of values,
therefore a distinctive ritual. Hence this final stage of manipulation tends to be the most alienating of all, since it is,
perhaps unwittingly, a celebration of one's own rootlessness.

*The rejection of traditional ritual places the individual
outside his community and is hence an alienating experience;
it tends not toward an increase of happiness or meaning but
the reverse.*

Although the chronology cannot be established with precision, it appears that radical, unauthorized changes were

introduced into liturgical practice earlier than radical ideas began to surface in doctrine, ecclesiastical government, or morals. The basic rites were rejected or drastically rearranged for the most part before doubts about the historic reality of Christ's Resurrection, the Trinity, the divine nature of Jesus, the priesthood, religious vows, papal and episcopal authority, and the indissolubility of marriage came to be expressed. The symbolic coherence of Catholicism was first weakened or destroyed, and the actual fabric followed afterward. So also the exodus of substantial numbers of persons from the Church followed rather than preceded the attempts to make liturgy "relevant."

The official liturgy, as well as the various manifestations of folk piety, articulate and symbolize a total moral and religious order. Thus the apparent breakdown of that system of symbols—a breakdown which was abetted in many cases by those who were supposed to be the guardians of the ritual, the clergy—conveyed the symbolic message, only dimly understood at the conscious level, that all restraints were now removed. This message soon had repercussions not only in the symbolic life of the Church but in its actual life as well: priests who became laymen, and nuns who repudiated their vows; laymen who rejected all religious authority on moral questions; radical changes of lifestyle everywhere in the Church. Religious communities which had been notoriously strict attempted to modernize almost instantaneously. Colleges which had been bastions of a genteel folk Catholicism suddenly proclaimed their secularity. Individuals who had been deeply involved in Church work gave it all up. Apparently quite stable marriages were dissolved as the former partners discovered their need to find themselves. There was a desacralization not only of the ritual but of man as well, as enlightened Catholics hastened to adopt a utilitarian secular ethic which could permit birth control, divorce, abortion, or sex outside marriage. It came to be seen as a dubious proposition that Catholics either have or should have a distinctive moral outlook. The eclecticism of experimental liturgy became an apt symbolization of the enlightened Catholic's merging into the secular moral consensus. Avant-garde liturgies tended to focus on moral issues of current concern in the enlightened secular world, with readings and music from similarly current sources.

Mary Douglas has discussed the connection between an individual's sense of his relation to his own body and his relation to the larger body of society. An acceptance of the need for bodily control is related to an acceptance of the need for strong social organization. A penchant for social disorder may also correspond to a sense of one's alienation from his own body, which can manifest itself in a carelessness about dress and diet and a search for altered states of consciousness, especially through drugs. This alienation can take religious form in a rejection, within Catholicism, of the belief in Christ's bodily presence in the Eucharist, followed by a skepticism about the Incarnation as well.[15] (Skepticism about the Incarnation has not, in recent years, taken the Docetic form of doubting that Jesus was really a man but the Arian form of doubting that He could have been fully divine.)

In accordance with this analysis it is significant that one of the basic doctrines on which the Liturgical Movement built for so many decades—the Mystical Body of Christ—also fell into general neglect during the era of experimentation. The sense of unity felt by the liturgical innovators was an altogether more secular and fragile thing than is expressed in that powerful image. Its decline corresponded also to a new sense of personal liberation which included giving free play to bodily needs, the rejection of strict sexual morality, benign approval of the casual hippie lifestyle, and at least a cautious neutrality toward drugs, with the willingness even to admit that they might be of some value in worship. The thirst for mystical experiences came to have nonreligious drives behind it, especially the desire to experience extreme states of consciousness which the mystics themselves had generally pronounced dangerous and inauthentic. The new sense of bodily liberation was also reflected in the new approach to worship in which the careful discipline imposed on the body in traditional liturgy gave way to a deliberate casualness, a desire to be spontaneous in gesture and posture as well as in sentiment.

Ironically, although the liturgical avant-garde talked much about community, in the end it was revealed that they were radical individualists, unconcerned about whatever community did exist in the Church and inclined to pursue policies which had the effect of weakening it still further. The notion that man's sense of God is primarily transmitted through the special forms and traditions of a particular people, or that one's moral perspective is achieved first of all in the same way, was implicitly ignored in their calculations. The worshiping community, for all the weight put on that concept, came to be a rather fragile gathering of radical individualists, and the difficulty of devising truly relevant liturgy stemmed from the fact that the personal needs and perspectives of the members of these groups were so diverse. The infinite complexity of existing communities, their dependence on tradition, on common ritual, on implicit understandings, was not basically respected.

The new emphasis on community was essentially on community defined as a narrow and relatively homogeneous group. A renewed liturgy which was supposed to deepen love in the Church ended frequently enough in diverse people who were formerly able to worship together finding that now they could worship only with persons like themselves. In many parishes there came to be the "guitar Mass" for the progressives and the "silent Mass" for the traditionalists. Numerous persons quit their parishes altogether to seek out small groups of like-minded souls. Extreme traditionalists went into schism. Liturgical theorists suggested that the territorial parish was dead, precisely because people could not worship together merely on the basis of happening to live near each other. Special parishes for students and professors, lawyers, social workers, etc., were proposed. Another principle had been defined:

The destruction of sacred ritual inhibits diverse kinds of people from participating in common worship by virtue of shared transcendental beliefs, and reduces community to scattered groups held together by limited concerns of a naturalistic kind.

The drive for spontaneity in worship was a reflection of this fragmentation of community. In the pre-reformed liturgy the sense of community which permitted diverse kinds of people to worship together, usually with little personal knowledge of one another, was a strong sense of a common past, a strong loyalty to a common set of sacred symbols, and a deep implicit awareness of the purpose of the ritual. This was objective community held together by bonds of iron, a community uniting living and dead in allegiance to certain basic beliefs and symbols. The new emphasis on community shifted to a subjective experience of community rather than its objective reality. The manipulation of the symbols, and the evident revolution in belief which was occurring, destroyed much of the objective character of the community, as it found itself suffering under growing polarization and confusion. A subjective experience of community was thus a necessary substitute. Reluctant worshipers in the parishes were exhorted to pray and sing together, exchange the sign of peace warmly and enthusiastically, and try to experience "true community," while unofficial groups tried all means of stimulating this experience through planned rites.

The need to stimulate a subjective sense of warmth and community in small groups is dictated by the weakening of the larger objective community and cannot adequately replace this larger community.

Sustaining this subjective sense of community requires constantly renewed and extended efforts, but such communities tend to be fragile and of relatively short duration.

The process of sustaining a subjective sense of community in small groups further weakens the larger community by emphasizing whatever is unique, personal, and unusual in the small group, that which by definition cannot be communicated adequately to the larger group. Simultaneously the beliefs and symbols of the larger group are further appropriated by the small group for its own uses.

Despite first appearances, it came to be clear after some years of liturgical experimentation that, weakened though they were, the communities which were the established parishes and the community which was the whole Church (dismissed often by radicals as merely the "institutional Church") were stronger and more viable than the great majority of the small groups formed on the basis of what appeared to be close personal affinity and common concerns.

To the degree that a traditional community is able to maintain a sense of its past and its inherited symbols, it will retain vitality, albeit in a possibly weakened state.

Ecclesiastical reformers were concerned, following the Second Vatican Council, that Catholics move beyond the "ghetto" of the Church and into the larger world, usually without noticing that the Catholic Church is perhaps the largest "ghetto" in the world, much larger and more diverse in its membership than any "worldly" group. However, here as elsewhere a notable irony developed: those who left the ghettos of the parishes to become part of the larger world often ended by joining even smaller and narrower ghettos than those from which they had liberated themselves—underground church groups, encounter groups, political sects, etc.

There is a natural human tendency to affiliate with specialized groups, and the rejection of one ghetto for the sake of achieving unity with all mankind is likely to end in the establishment of newer ghettos at least as restricted as the one first rejected.

Mary Douglas has discerned three stages in the development of religion which are directly applicable to the recent history of the Catholic Church. In the first, which never applied to the Church as a whole but did apply to the majority of its members through most of its history, theological belief is implicit only, there is fixed ritual, and sin is regarded as specific immoral acts. In the second, which describes the general historical character of the Church, theology becomes explicit, ritual is still fixed, and sin is still specific actions. In the final stage there is a tendency to disregard theology, spontaneous acts replace fixed ritual, and sin is conceived as improper attitudes, of which specific acts are merely manifestations. As the society loses its grip on the individual (here the society which is the Church), there is a renewal of romanticism, especially a great emphasis on the virtues of sincerity and honesty.[16]

Theology has not of course been abandoned in the contemporary Church, but there has been a growing reluctance to define beliefs, a tendency to permit a wide range of vague understandings (of the meaning of the Eucharist, for example), and in neo-Pentecostalism a resurgence of a nontheological piety in which religious feeling is primarily valued. The precipitous decline in the practice of confession by

Catholics can almost certainly be traced to a new attitude toward morality which denigrates the importance of specific, numerable acts and to a new cult of spontaneity which views the rite of confession as merely formal and hence of no value (although confessors who probe deeply into the penitent's moral life may find that this does not serve to make the experience more attractive either). Since the practice of confession has for many centuries been close to the center of Catholic piety, this is a crucial case of the inherent opposition between traditional Catholic life and the new cultural attitudes abroad in the Church.

The decline in the practice of confession—a ritualized, austere, and private form of self-revelation—is especially curious given the concomitant rise in popularity of other kinds of self-disclosure like encounter groups. The rejection of confession by so many advanced Catholics perhaps derives specifically from the fact that confession is a submission of the individual to the authority of the whole Church, an acknowledgment of offenses designated as sinful by that Church, and a forgiveness offered by the Church. Its rejection is, in other words, a rejection of the authority of the Church over one's life, an assertion once again of the claims of radical individualism, manifested also in the denial by so many former priests and nuns of the authority of vows (promises to God made in the presence of the whole Church) or by some lay people of the necessity of a ritual marriage ceremony or the permanent character of marital vows.

That the systematic encouragement of personal expression, without any corresponding ritual acceptance of the demands of a society, tends toward the breakdown of all communal bonds is evident in the history of many encounter groups, including for example those conducted within religious communities, where the expression of members' "true" feelings has sometimes resulted in hostilities and psychic wounds which made further community life all but impossible. (One well-known order of nuns which undertook prolonged encounter experiences suffered an irreconcilable schism within its ranks and lost the majority of its members.[17])

The encounter-group rationale is merely a distillation and a refinement of an attitude which tends toward being pervasive in American society, which underlies the antiritual attitude, and which has also the tendency to undermine all stable community life. It has been described as follows:

. . . the predication of an essentially positive "real self" or "inner nature" which in the healthy person resists the imposition of social roles. Social relations, the family especially, either allow the self to develop naturally or layer upon it artificial identities, but in no case do they form or alter its essential nature. . . . Change comes from within and to this process of self-actualization man owes his first allegiance. . . . Spontaneity is an important value because through it the self demonstrates its freedom from external conditioning. The exigencies of spontaneous self-actualization might have untoward consequences on the people around us but these secondary effects must be given a back seat to the primary right to grow. In any case, one need not worry overmuch because, since one's inner nature is inherently good, whatever is genuinely part of its unfolding can give little reason for concern. The Kingdom of Heaven is within each person.

. . . Since he [man] is passionately committed to the primary importance of his own autonomy, it is even difficult to understand why he would be interested in a group in the first place, unless mainly as an arena for the emprise of his will. One cannot help sensing here the pathos and irony of trying to extract the gratifications of community from experience based on a dressed-up version of the old gospel of individualism. The one simply cannot be produced from the other, and in the desperation of the attempt it is possible to glimpse how keen must be the isolation of the individual supposed to be experiencing intimacy within the group. . . .

. . . The web of social roles that he [the individual] finds himself ensnared in at present cannot be regarded as other than external to his being: the struggle to disentangle and cultivate his real self. Thus his "role" as parent, teacher, writer, social worker, Christian or Jew, is important only in a secondary way and does not have to be submitted to careful scrutiny. . . . For such an individual . . . learning to block out the external pressures . . . is a process not often conducive to distinguishing between the claims of social conformity and the claims of ethical or religious imperatives—they both come from the outside.[18]

All of this can perhaps yield a few additional principles:

The established ritual of a community reflects among other things the ways in which the competing claims of common traditions and the desires of the various members have been negotiated and reconciled.

A strong sense of conflict between the demands of the traditions and the needs of the individual is evidence of the radical breakdown of the spirit of community, and attempts to ease the conflict through radical alteration of the traditions merely tend to hasten the community's actual dissolution.

The breakdown of these communal bonds tends to validate expressions of unchecked egotism.

NOTES

1. Patrick Regan, O.S.B., "The Change behind the Changes," *Worship*, XL, 1 (January, 1966), p. 38.
2. *Natural Symbols*, pp. 1–2, 8, 11, 47.
3. *Ibid.*, pp. 49–51.
4. *Ibid.*, pp. 9, 38.
5. Geertz, "Ritual and Social Change: a Javanese Example," *American Anthropologist*, XLIX, 1 (February, 1957), pp. 32–54.

6. *Natural Symbols,* pp. 13–14, 19, 30, 33, 55, 139, 141.

7. *The Sacred Canopy: Elements of a Sociological Theory of Religion* (Garden City, N.Y., 1967), pp. 40, 50.

8. *Magic, Science, and Religion* (Garden City, N.Y., 1955), p. 67.

9. "Passages, Margins, and Poverty," *Worship,* XLVI, 7 (September, 1972), p. 398.

10. "Religion as a Cultural System," *The Religious Situation: 1968,* ed. Donald R. Cutler (Boston, 1968), p. 659.

11. Reported by Adolph Schalk, "A Mixed Picture," *Commonweal,* May 25, 1973, p. 287.

12. " 'Rite of Divorce' Enacted during Mass," *The National Catholic Reporter,* November 3, 1972, p. 17.

13. DeJong, "Liturgical Developments in Holland," *Liturgy in Transition,* ed. H. Schmidt (*Concilium,* LXII [1971]), p. 148.

14. Sonya Rudikoff, "Marriage and Household," *Commentary,* June, 1973, p. 59.

15. *Natural Symbols,* pp. 64–65, 160–61, 165.

16. *Ibid.,* pp. 31, 35.

17. The Immaculate Heart Sisters of Los Angeles. See the account by William R. Coulson, *Groups, Gimmicks, and Instant Gurus, an Examination of Encounter Groups and Their Distortions* (New York, 1972), pp. 99, 130–31, 147.

18. Alan L. Mintz, "Encounter Groups and Other Panaceas," *Commentary,* July, 1973, pp. 48–49.

CHAPTER 6

Folk Religion

From the beginning advocates of liturgical change recognized two principal sources of opposition: the hierarchy and older clergy most of whom had shown little enthusiasm for the Liturgical Movement even at its most moderate, and the masses of lay people who seemed inordinately attached to traditional ways. (There was not even much agitation for the vernacular outside the circles of professional liturgists.) The Second Vatican Council witnessed a remarkable shift on the part of the bishops, who rather unexpectedly accepted almost the whole program of the Liturgical Movement, although few bishops gave any support to the radical experiments which followed. Lay people remained a problem, although there was a gradual acceptance of the new ways and even, after a while, limited enthusiasm.

The process of liturgical change laid bare the largest contradiction in the whole of renewal, however, in that a keynote of the new Church was supposed to be the rights of the laity; yet in this as in other matters few laity were consulted as to their wishes, and lay resistance to change was dealt with by a combination of condescending persuasion and authoritarian commands.

Thomas Merton had warned about "the type of zeal which does great harm to the liturgy. It is what makes the simple and ordinary Christian afraid of Liturgy with a capital L," and which made popular devotions more important to many people than the Mass itself.[1] A prominent priest-liturgist rejoiced during the Council that reformers had chosen not to attack popular devotions, vulnerable though they were to criticism, but he warned that the Liturgical Movement's chief danger, on the eve of its victory, was the temptation to compromise, which he thought it would resist because it was "too old and too wise to indulge in half-hearted measures or compromise proposals." He saw in the liturgists a "praiseworthy devotion to truth and freedom, to a reasonable and equitable solution," but felt that through a desire to accommodate every legitimate claim, "having scrupulously avoided any apparent excess or extreme," they would destroy their own bargaining position. Those who favored the vernacular, for example, had bent over backward to reassure those who favored Latin. They did not demand that "every syllable of public prayer should be in the language of the one praying." He found little desire to reform the Roman Canon; at best minor changes were needed. But he warned that even moderate changes might be rejected if liturgists were not bold enough.[2]

A future president of the Liturgical Conference took occasion, at the 1963 Liturgical Week, to praise the new catechists for their moderation and charity, concluding that "If they must bear witness to a truth which is not fully known by all, they do so gently, lest they trip up their brother." But six years later, following the final Liturgical Week in Milwaukee, he was driven to dismiss his critics as "stiff-assed honkies."[3] In retrospect an executive secretary of the Conference recalled that liturgists had put up a moderate front, thinking "Don't alienate the skittish bishops, now that we want their votes."[4]

As the new rites were in the process of being introduced, a priest-liturgist prominent in the Conference published an enthusiastic exposition of their benefits, showing in detail their superiority to the old ways. In the process he ridiculed traditionalists, whose principal motivation he thought could only be insecurity. He compared liturgists to health officers sent into the tropics by colonial governments and wondered whether the natives would have sense enough to listen for their own good. Warming to his theme, he asserted boldly that those who resisted the new rites "in a very important sense, don't matter. (Everyone matters tremendously, of course; we mean their concerns are ultimately not important ones.) God can save the worriers and bring them to heaven somehow." Such people, he thought, had "nothing vital to say." Although professing his respect for the "genius and talents of all people," he also expressed regret at the popularity of the cults of the saints among Catholics. Finally, in case persuasion alone had not been enough to convince the skeptics, he reminded his readers that, as to the new liturgy, "It's the Law!" and concluded by recalling Christ's words "If you love me keep my commandments." Later he was to confess that the laity frightened him, and he recorded his impression that each Sunday thousands of people trooped into the churches to participate in "nothing!" [5]

Before long the laity, with their ingrained habits of piety, began to seem almost like the enemy. A church architect urged that churches be built without side chapels so that people would be discouraged from engaging in private prayer. He also thought it was wrong to put the altar at the center of the church because other activities are just as important as what occurs at the holy table.[6] Sounding what quickly became a major theme of radical reformers, a lawyer told the 1966 Liturgical Week that the people in suburban parishes were in love with banalities and fleeing from life. Such parishes were at best "harmless rest camps," although "social psychologists see the flight to insulated residential areas . . . in pathological terms." Suburbanites were characterized as courting amnesia, and he expressed fear lest special liturgical groups of, for example, bankers be formed, since such people were incapable of understanding the gospel.[7] As already noted, other prominent liturgists were condemning the people's proclivities toward "magic," dismissing them as unchristian, characterizing their piety as "senile," and charging that they worshiped the rites themselves, not the God of the rites

In time the major official changes, especially the vernacular itself, came to be accepted by most of the laity. Resistance to liturgical change, especially unauthorized and radical experiments, was motivated not only by the unfamiliarity of the innovations, however, but also by the accurate perception by many of the laity that such experiments were directed at them as subjects, victims, or enemies. The innovators believed something was radically wrong with the Catholic Church, and what they increasingly decided was principally wrong was the people themselves and their benighted attitudes. Liturgy, far from achieving peace and community in the Church, became a growing source of irritation and strife not only because its new diversity reflected and promoted disunity but because the drive for change was seen to proceed from a deep contempt for the mainstream of the Church. The wells were poisoned almost from the beginning.

The criticisms which liturgists directed at popular Catholicism were varied and at least to some degree valid. They charged that it obscured the importance of the Mass behind a plethora of noneucharistic devotions, that the latter were frequently dubious from a theological standpoint and even unintentionally heretical, that most of the laity failed to appreciate the deep significance of many of the rites, that these rites were sometimes entered into with a passive and magical attitude, and that much of popular piety was sentimental and in bad taste. In justifying the liturgical changes reformers appealed ceaselessly to the authority of the Second Vatican Council, and official sanctions (including excommunication) were invoked against those who clung to the old ways. Ceaseless appeal was also made to the example of the early Church, to which all the innovations were supposedly designed to return.

The actual development of liturgical change, as distinct from its theoretical justification, soon indicated, however, that innovators were inclined to indulge almost without end their own evolving tastes, while continuing to keep a rather tight rein on conservatives. (Amid all the talk about "liturgical pluralism," no prominent reformer proposed authorizing the Mass of Pius V for those who were willing even to endure excommunication in order to keep it.)

Popular devotions were pruned to allow the Mass to stand out in unhidden glory. In many parishes, despite what the Vatican Council had advised, priests simply suppressed novenas, removed statues which had been the focus of popular cults, stopped celebrating Benediction of the Blessed Sacrament, and refused to reintroduce them when asked by parishioners. Priests who, in this atmosphere, hung banners proclaiming "Peace" and "Love" in the churches could not understand why these were sometimes interpreted as acts of aggression. Numerous sermons were preached instructing the faithful on the shallowness of their religious attitudes, although the preachers themselves had been among those encouraging such attitudes a short time before. Within four years of the Council a liturgist could note somewhat sadly that there had been a precipitous and measurable decline in all devotional practices, and no evident substitutes were forthcoming. (Such things as Bible vigils generally failed to take hold.) He noted that a whole way of life had been undermined, and that it had been done in the name of the liturgy.[8]

All this might have been to the good if it had indeed led to a revitalized eucharistic piety. But among those who liked the new liturgy least were many who had been intensely devoted to the Mass all their lives, had risen early almost every day of the year to get to Communion, and were now sometimes treated by the clergy as problem cases, fanatics to be humored. (Especially distasteful to the liturgists was such people's lack of enthusiasm for singing and praying in unison at 6 A.M.) Mass attendance fell off steadily and measurably in the years following the Council. Most significantly, liturgists themselves began to show evident doubts about the importance of the Mass. Many of those who had most ardently supported the official changes expressed keen disappointment with the results and set out to look for congenial experimental celebrations. Among advanced liturgists, the central importance of the Eucharist was not quite denied, but its significance became less and less clear, interpretations of it became more and more diverse, its structure was increasingly subject to alteration, and in some experimental groups it was definitely shoved into the background. Its primacy over other devotions had been based on the belief that it was the sacrifice of the body and blood of Christ; if it was now to be primarily a celebration of human community it was not at all clear why other celebrations were not equally important.

In criticizing popular piety from a theological standpoint, the Liturgical Movement, in this as in other ways, had sought to promote an increase of orthodoxy in the Church, the suppression even of innocent and unconscious heresy. Those who heard themselves called material heretics, however, discovered before long that orthodoxy was not at all the keynote of the advanced reformers, that they were prepared to tolerate all manner of diverse theological opinion and even to obliterate the category of heresy altogether. Experimental Eucharists became a major forum for the exposition of daring theological opinions. Those who had ceaselessly reminded the laity of their obligation to follow the decrees of the Council now often prided themselves on their own defiance of the hierarchy, including the pope, and sometimes dismissed the Second Vatican Council as rather limited and irrelevant in its concerns and certainly as lacking in any ultimate authority.

Although originally patronized for their lack of appreciation of the depths of liturgical riches found in the Church, many laymen soon discovered that liturgists themselves were routinely pronouncing much of this richness "meaningless" and "irrelevant." Although advanced priests and laymen in private sometimes ridiculed elderly widows for their "magical beliefs," an even more blatant interest in magic was treated with respect when sophisticated college students took it up a few years later. (A Dominican theologian, while approving the demythologizing of Catholic liturgy which had taken place, also bestowed his blessing on various of the fashionable new occult "churches." [9])

In one area especially, sophisticated reformers ought to have had unimpeachable credentials: artistic significance and good taste. Thomas Merton had been especially strong in denouncing a popular religious art which led away "from the realm of intuition and of mystery into the more superficial level of sentimental fantasy." He added:

. . . subjective emotionalism tends to lessen the true force of the symbol of the cross, and to create a diversion in favor of dramatic appeal which is not universal. It may strongly affect certain types and temperaments, but it will also, by this very fact, distract or even repel others of diverse character. It is precisely this emotional tone of subjectivity which paves the way for caricature.

But our liturgical designers, including perhaps chiefly those most innocent and fervent of them, the sisters, have ingenuously adopted the advertising technique. . . .

No one could have foreseen when these words were written that as liturgical "reform" gathered steam fashionable nuns, now perhaps a little less innocent and fervent, would quite consciously and deliberately produce religious art copied from advertising (Wonder Bread, United Air Lines, Hallmark Cards), which would be hung on chapel walls all over the country. Other of the new banners eschewed religious symbolism for hortatory and "inspirational" sayings, like "Remember that today is the first day of the rest of your life," just as Father Merton had warned:

Hence the liturgical "illustration" and "decoration" is to advertise certain possibilities of emotional satisfaction which we can make our own if we go to work and stir up the appropriate affections in the depths of our own soul. . . .

I do not deny that there are some people for whom this may work. But I question the fact that it is the full and true traditional function of sacred art.

On the contrary I think it represents a degradation and an impoverishment of Christian symbolism. I think it makes art a destructive and dissipating force. . . .[10]

These remarks, which crystallized much of the liturgical thinking immediately before the Second Vatican Council, applied to the popular religious art of an earlier day, much of which the reformers soon succeeded in sweeping away. Yet they remained equally applicable after the Vatican Council, when innovators either introduced a new emotionalism and a new sentimentality into worship or watched benignly while others introduced it. There was a great eagerness to approve guitar masses, for example, as constituting a decided improvement over the music of the past. Many

Catholics ceased ever to hear the Divine Praises, the *Angelus*, the *Regina Coeli*, or the *Salve Regina*, but the pseudo-poetry of Rod McKuen or Kahlil Gibran was sometimes introduced into the Mass. Popular old hymns, especially Marian hymns, were effectively banned as shallow and sentimental, only to be replaced by such new standards as *Allelu!, Here We Are All Together!, Sons of God, Take Our Bread We Ask You,* and *What a Great Thing It Is!* Worshipers were invited in song to "Come away" to a place where "The land is flowing with all riches" and "Happiness and other such wishes." To get there "Just take my hand and you're half way there now," so that "Side by side we'll walk together" and "all the way we'll love one another." The very concept of good taste seemed to drop from the reformers' minds, as everything was now justified in proportion as "the people want it." It was becoming clear, however, who "the people" were.

The whole process of liturgical reform was so replete with ironies that it is impossible to notice all of them. It had been professional liturgists who had insisted that Gregorian Chant was the only music truly acceptable for worship, and professional liturgists who all but banned it from the churches. It was professional liturgists who condemned popular hymns for their superficiality and sentiment, and professional liturgists who lent their authority to the new forms of superficiality and sentiment. It was professional liturgists who had flogged ordinary churchgoers for not appreciating the rituals enough, and professional liturgists who pronounced these same rituals outmoded.

In retrospect it is clear that from the beginning liturgical reform was an enterprise carried out with a rather limited clientele in mind—well-educated and relatively sophisticated persons. It was they who, in the 1940s and 1950s, appreciated the purity of chant, the majesty of the traditional ritual, and the subtle theories of Casel, Otto, and Eliade. As late as 1965 solemn Latin High Masses were attracting crowds of intellectuals and students in such places as Cambridge, Massachusetts, and New Haven, Connecticut. It was this same clientele who, far more than the ordinary Catholic, longed for prayer and song in common and, finally, for the vernacular. It was they who, about 1966, began to reject the organ for the guitar, solemnity for spontaneity, tradition for experimentation. At each stage of the Liturgical Movement the desires of these kinds of people were interpreted as expressing the authentic will of the Church. The masses of uneducated were always deemed deficient in taste, whether from a failure to appreciate the beauties of chant or a stubborn penchant for appreciating them too much. Yet the educated and sophisticated for whose sakes the reforms were made were soon enough dissatisfied with them also. The vernacular, congregational participation, the priest facing the people, lay lectors, Offertory processions, and guitar music were after all not enough.

In a passing remark near the beginning of the Council, H. A. Reinhold had observed that the Germans and Slavs had traditions of congregational singing which the Irish and Italians did not, and thought this was one reason the new ways were slow in catching on.[11] It was a more significant comment than he knew at the time, coming as it did nearly ten years before the advent of the "new ethnicity" in the American Church. Yet in retrospect it is also possible to see that Germans and Americans of German extraction always had a disproportionate influence in the Liturgical Movement and that the Movement had little tendency to respect the indigenous customs of the various Catholic peoples. The occasionally extravagant devotions of the Italians particularly suffered under this rigor. Paradoxically, when advanced reformers discovered in the later 1960s that spontaneity and celebration were supposed to be the hallmarks of good liturgy, they often invoked the tradition of *fiesta* which is found among the Latin peoples but not much among the

Germans, Irish, or English. Like the introduction of "folk" music into the liturgy, it was an attempt to impose on the people a "popular" idiom which had little to do with their own real customs. The liturgical tradition in the Western Church, among most peoples, is one of solemnity and deep reverence. In attempting to alter this to one of spontaneity and even playfulness, experimenters were necessarily doing violence to the fabric of liturgical life as it was actually lived. The symbolism of "folk liturgy" was often patently hollow: the blue-jeaned guitarist who attended the best college and drove a Jaguar, the pseudo-naïve lyrics sung by an informal choir of sophisticates, the words of love in the mouths of individuals who had strong feelings of animosity toward bourgeois society, the "people's songs" composed by professionals, the people's songbooks which warned the "people" against reproducing the texts without paying royalties to the publishers.

As concern for the Third World developed around 1970, liturgists began to recognize that native culture had often been treated cavalierly by missionaries and there was a new interest in incorporating native elements into worship. (One liturgist even thought ritual drunkenness might be compatible with the Eucharist.[12]) Yet it was merely a further irony, since those priests who talked so earnestly about the beauties of popular tradition in the Third World, of the arrogance that destroyed or weakened those traditions, were often among those who had shown the least sympathy for the traditions of their own people, had applauded and abetted the destruction of so much of Catholic folk piety in America.

A state almost of warfare between liturgists and people continued into the 1970s, when a dispute erupted between the Federation of Diocesan Liturgical Commissions and the Catholic Biblical Association over a proposal by the former group to exclude Scripture readings from printed missalettes distributed to worshipers. The liturgists complained that printed texts bind celebrants to fixed readings and argued that worshipers should listen to the Scripture being read, not read it themselves from the booklets. Although a national survey purported to show that a majority of parishes wanted the texts printed, the liturgists declared that such printed booklets were outdated, although "Most people don't realize this, and an educational program must now begin so that real participation can thrive and flourish." A spokesman for the Federation added that the national poll was invalid because people tended to vote for what they were familiar with. Meanwhile a pastor reported that he had solved the problem in his parish by hiding the missalettes from the people.[13] A prominent liturgist, noting that many Catholics decline to receive Communion in their hands because of their feelings about the sacredness of the act, argued that they should simply be instructed about the ignorance of their belief and informed that the Eucharist is "a bread which is broken to feed man's larger hungers." He ridiculed a suggestion that there be separate Communion lines for those following the traditional customs and added that "The only answer is a sensitive catechesis." [14]

Mary Douglas, in situating the liturgical crisis within the general cultural crisis of the time, discerned

. . . three phases in the move away from ritualism. First, there is the contempt of external ritual forms; second, there is the private internalising of religious experience; third, there is the move to humanist philanthropy. When the third stage is underway, the symbolic life of the spirit is finished. . . . The reformers set low value on the external and symbolic aspects of Friday abstinence and who exhort the faithful to prefer eleemosynary deeds are not making an intellectually free assessment of forms of worship. They are moving with the secular tide along with other sections of the middle class who seek to be justified in their lives only by saving others from hunger and injustice. . . .

The Friday abstainers are not free to follow their pastors in their wide-ranging philanthropy. For each person's religion has to do with himself and his own autonomous needs. There is a sad disjunction between the recognized needs of clergy, teachers, writers, and the needs of those they preach to and write for.

The final stage of the unraveling of ritual and community is that of the present, in which men are dominated by notions of personal success, doing good, professionalism, and a generalized guilt over social injustice. Professor Douglas concludes:

. . . those who are responsible for ecclesiastical decisions are only too likely to have been made, by the manner of their education, insensitive to non-verbal signals and dull to their meaning. This is central to the difficulties of Christianity today.[15]

The conflict between clergy and other professionals advocating "correct" forms of worship and masses of believers following their own customs is a perennial one in the Church. In Yucatán, for example, Robert Redfield found that the same villages were simultaneously the most Catholic and the most pagan. Catholic rites were regarded as the property of all the people, and there were periodic conflicts with reforming priests seeking to suppress pagan practices.[16] For the most part throughout the history of the Church the conflict has been muted by a broad tolerance of popular customs. Having conquered paganism in the early Middle Ages, the Church made its peace with it and allowed pagan remnants to exist within Catholic practice; some pagan elements were even deliberately claimed by the Church for its own use.

Periodically there have been strong manifestations of puritanism, of which the Reformation was the most notable. The Liturgical Movement following the Second Vatican Council has been the most significant expression of the puritan spirit within Catholicism in modern times, although like all puritanism it has tended to have an uneasy relationship with the Church. (Thomas Merton had noted before the Council that puritanism ". . . having first removed valid art and then permitted the substitution of more corrupt and popular forms, has paved the way for the degradation of sacred art by sentimentality." [17])

The attempt systematically to purify popular worship tends toward the destruction not only of the forms of piety but of the piety itself.

As a deeply ingrained and traditional piety is rooted out, the void will be filled not by a more authentic Christianity but by available resources provided by popular culture.

In particular the attack on popular devotions in the name of the Sacrifice of the Mass has led to a weakened regard for the latter as well.

In the words of Mary Douglas:

Perhaps it is true that Friday abstinence became a wall behind which the Catholics . . . retired too smugly. But it was the only ritual which brought Christian symbols down into the kitchen and larder and on to the dinner table in the manner of Jewish rules of impurity. To take away one symbol that meant something is no guarantee that the spirit of charity will flow in its place. It might have been safer to build upon that small symbolic wall in the hope that eventually it could come to surround Mount Sion.[18]

One of the more significant ironies of the period of reform was the fact that the priesthood was being demythologized at the same time the liturgy was in a state of flux, the two in obvious close relationship to each other. Yet the demythologizing of the priesthood was precisely the factor which enabled many of the laity to resist liturgical changes. At first they followed, somewhat unenthusiastically, reforms which they were told represented the recovery of a more authentic and ancient Catholic tradition. This was in fact true of most of the officially mandated changes. However, as liturgical experimentation proceeded, many laymen came to sense that they had a surer grasp on the meaning of the Church's traditions than did some of the specialists and that the demands of modern secular culture, not the ancient traditions of the Church, were guiding much of the new liturgical activity. They were at this point able psychologically to oppose further experiments, sometimes to denounce priests to those in higher authority (who were often in turn reluctant to act on these lay complaints), and even in extreme cases to go into schism. They sensed that, as liturgists sometimes asserted, liturgy belongs to the whole Church and the whole people have responsibility for it. They extended the principle, however, to include the idea that professional liturgists have no special authority if they depart from the authentic spirit of the Church. The laity began to assert their rights in ways progressive clergy had not anticipated.

Catholic folk religion over the centuries has had striking resemblances to the folk religion found in many otherwise diverse cultures. There is an evident disjunction between "transcendental" and "pragmatic" religion, the latter of which leans heavily on fixed rites and concerns itself to a great extent with concrete goals, particularly the appropriation of divine power for the sake of healing or other material benefits. This appropriation is one important way by which the dichotomy of sacred and profane is bridged. Formal education tends to inspire opposition to pragmatic religion in the name of a purer transcendental faith.[19]

At its worst, folk Catholicism tends toward an unabashed paganism. It follows the pattern, noticed by Eliade and others, whereby the "high god" of a people is gradually forgotten as he is elevated so far above the world as to have no influence on it, and lesser divinities are worshiped in practice. Religion then becomes more carnal and more selfish, although also more human.[20] The great pioneer psychologist of religion William James stated bluntly that "The religion of the common people has always been polytheism,"[21] and at certain times and places the Catholic saints have in fact functioned as minor deities in competition with God himself.[22]

Liturgical reformers were always keenly aware of the impurity of so much folk Catholicism, although in the urbanized Western countries there has been a much closer connection between popular cults and official piety than in peasant societies. The liturgists' puritanical attacks on this folk piety were odd from several points of view, however. It was particularly strange that in the America of the 1960s, amid an evidently growing and militant secularism, superstition and magic should have been deemed such severe dangers to the Church. The contemporary atmosphere would seem to make a tolerance of superstitious excess permissible in the Church, since the force of the surrounding culture constantly works against such things. Instead liturgists chose to direct much of their energy into combating the semipagan excesses of folk piety, while simultaneously opening themselves more and more to the sophisticated high paganism of, for example, Bernstein's *Mass* or other syncretic and eccentric uses of traditional liturgy. Their sometimes fierce opposition to folk piety was also odd given their general lack of concern about neo-magic as it came to birth among sophisticates. People who saw something pernicious in novenas were often prepared to smile tolerantly at a newly fashionable astrology.

Perhaps oddest of all was the fact that liturgical reform originally aimed at recalling Catholics from "pragmatic" to "transcendental" religion, from a piety too much given over to petitionary invocations and thanksgiving for favors and back to a pure worship of God. Yet the destruction of the patterns of folk piety was followed by a new interest on the part of liturgists themselves in "relevant" worship directly related to the needs of the human community. In folk Catholicism, however, the more blatantly self-concerned forms of religion had been satisfactorily controlled by limiting them primarily to noneucharistic devotions. Now, in the reformed liturgical economy, the Mass itself was systematically reshaped by the liturgical avant-garde to render it usable for the narrow purposes of specific groups. Its function as a great act of pure worship declined accordingly, and some people professed to find the entire notion of transcendental worship meaningless.

The attempt to make worship "pure" often masks hidden discontents with the very act of worship and may be the step prior to the discovery of its "irrelevance" even in its purified state.

Perhaps no concern has so dominated advanced liturgical thought since the Council as the determination to deny any vestige of connection between Catholic liturgy and magic. Yet the denial is not convincing unless traditional rites are either eliminated altogether or reinterpreted in ways almost unrecognizable from the standpoint of traditional belief. If the liturgy is, as classical thought insisted, a great divine mystery, then it will inevitably have magical connotations for some people; the Church can seek to control these but cannot hope to eliminate them. In seeking to eliminate them, radical liturgists have necessarily humanized the ritual to the point where it no longer has any magical connotations principally because it has so few connotations of divinity.

In any religion which esteems ritual, it has been found virtually impossible to draw a sharp and convincing distinction between religion and magic. What is a pure religious act from one point of view may be viewed magically from another. The distinction between the two is clear if polar phenomena are studied: a profound mystical experience, on the one hand, versus a simple primitive spell, on the other. But inevitably the two sides meet at some point, and it is the area of their meeting which causes the definitional problem. Magic and religion are probably best seen as forming a continuum.[23] As Bronislaw Malinowski warned, it is also a mistake to interpret magic too simply—even primitive people have a knowledge of the "natural" world and can function effectively as "secular" men. Magical rites have limited purposes and are not as irrational as may first appear.[24]

Several important principles derive from this:

Historically Catholicism has accommodated itself more to the magical, primitively pagan tendencies of human culture than to puritanism, sensing that puritanism is often a prelude to secularization.

The scientific mentality is not in necessary opposition to a belief in ritual efficacy, since even primitive people are capable of distinguishing what is purely "natural" from what is effected by ritual action.

The attempt to eliminate all element of "magic" from liturgy tends to lead to its secularization.

In various parts of the world it has been discovered that the practice of illegitimate magic, especially witchcraft, increases as traditional religion declines. Magic tends to flourish as a result of rapid and disintegrating social change and may be more common at the "advanced" and urbanized end of the social spectrum than at the rural end.[25] This sociological principle received abundant confirmation in the years during which the liturgy of the Catholic Church appeared in such disarray. Nothing surprised reformers more than "secular man's" sudden turn to astrology, satanism, witch-

craft, and other varieties of supposedly outmoded superstition. One explanation popular in progressive circles was that
the Church itself, by its emphasis on ritual and "externals,"
had stimulated a perverse interest in magic.[26] What such an
explanation missed was the formidable persistence of magical attitudes throughout the world's history, in all cultures
and all ages. The anxieties and hopes which give rise to
magical belief appear to be indigenous to human nature and,
although they can be muted and suppressed for a time, re-
assert themselves periodically.

*The benign ritual of the Catholic Church is perhaps the
most effective antidote to magic to have evolved in Western
culture because, instead of denying the reality of magic and
the anxieties which give rise to it, this ritual counters them
in their own terms.*

*The weakening of traditional sacred symbols and tradi-
tional systems of meaning tends to stimulate belief in magic,
as anxious individuals search for new protection against the
suddenly revealed chaos of the universe.*

Besides its magical accretions, what liturgical reformers
found most objectionable in folk piety was its apparent
meaninglessness, especially the people's mode of participation in the Mass itself—passive, silent, uncomprehending,
uninvolved. The major thrust of liturgical change was that
of bringing the Mass to the people, allowing them to participate in an enlightened and educated way.

Although there were powerful arguments in favor of these
reforms, liturgists tended to overlook one significant fact:
the passive worshiper in the pew seemed to have a profound
sense of the Mass's importance, attended Mass with a sense
of reverence, and sometimes went to great length to do so
(for example, those individuals who, although they may
have prayed their rosaries instead of their missals, walked

through snow at 6 A.M. to attend Mass before going to work).

All things being equal it is obvious that educated participation in a comprehensible rite is preferable to a piety which is hazy even if devout. However, efforts to make the Mass "meaningful" were not self-evidently successful, judging by the decline of church attendance and the swelling complaints of its irrelevance, which followed rather than preceded the reforms. Many individuals who had joined in the Latin Mass without serious complaint stopped attending after the reforms were complete, or found "meaningful" liturgy only in experimental small groups. While the gains from liturgical reform probably outweigh the losses, the balance is perhaps more nearly equal than liturgists are prepared to recognize.

One of the liturgists' major errors was what might be called the "fallacy of explicitness." It was the assumption that a symbol or an experience cannot be meaningful unless its meaning can be articulated verbally and coherently. Given this assumption, uneducated Catholics were virtually doomed to being regarded as inferior, since most of them lacked the ability to articulate their feelings adequately and could not be expected to master a complex symbolology.

Emile Durkheim proposed that the true significance of religious rites lies not in the specific goals they purportedly aim at but in their general spiritual effect on the participants, which is often inexpressible.[27] Members of primitive tribes are found to entertain the most diverse and even contradictory notions of the meaning of their various rituals, with only a few select individuals fully in command of the lore behind them.[28] The anthropologist Clyde Kluckhohn has described the uncertain relationship which exists between "myth" and "ritual," the former the official account adopted by a people to explain the latter. Sometimes they exist independent of one another; sometimes rituals are practiced which have no myths to explain them.[29] In the history of

the Catholic Church the majority of membership has existed at a very low level of education, so that a sophisticated
understanding of ritual could not reasonably be expected.
(The maligned traditional catechisms were an attempt to
provide as much of this as possible.) For probably most
Catholics, even at the present time, the meaning of the sacred rites has existed at a level beneath that of explicit
verbal formulation.

The Second Vatican Council, so dominated by the prelates
and theologians of the northwestern part of the globe, perceived that the Church was at an important historic water-
shed in part because in the most "progressive" countries
mass education had reached the point where some other
form of liturgical participation might be possible. The momentous decisions to translate the liturgy into the vernacular, encourage informed lay participation, and simplify the
ritual were recognitions of this new situation.

In a culture where people are capable of being instructed
and expect some rationale for everything they do, it would
be obscurantist to try to preserve a pseudo-peasant culture
of implicit meanings. But one of the great errors of liturgical
reform was the fact that the new ways were so often justified through denigrating the old. This in turn engendered a
good deal of bitterness, resistance, and suspicion. It demor-
alized people who were made to feel that all their lives they
had not been praying properly, that there was something
profoundly flawed about their faith. It placed a premium on
change and discontinuity, whereas liturgical reform would
have been most effective if reformers had built on existing
traditions as much as possible.

Most serious, however, was the previously mentioned fallacy of explicitness. With the commendable goal of elevating
worshipers' conscious awareness of the meaning of the ritual,
many liturgists all but denied that the rites could have implicit meanings not exhaustible by verbal formulas. To a great

extent they forgot how liturgy has functioned in the historical church. They were eager to pronounce "meaningless"
rites which countless millions had for centuries joined in
with great reverence, which had formed and sustained many
great saints, which had seemed so important to Catholics
that they had risked their lives to celebrate them in time of
persecution, to bring them onto the battlefield, even under
the most difficult of circumstances to perform them in prison
camps. Here was found, at a minimum, the powerful "con-
densed symbol" described by Mary Douglas: a timeless act
which summed up the whole moral and spiritual existence
of the participant, which joined God and man in profound
unity. At a minimum the old Mass created an atmosphere
where prayer was encouraged, even if it was private prayer.

On one level traditional ritual gave to worshipers a strong
sense of belonging, whose meaning was in essence "I participate; therefore I am." Specific meanings were subordinated to the sense of general membership in a mystical
community.[30] Through that sense of belonging, deeper and
more enduring than the more conscious experiences of community fostered in the new liturgy, a whole range of values
and a whole way of life were intuited. Hence a visible
change in this ritual provoked fears (justified, as it turned
out) that these values and this way of life were in danger
of being undermined. The experience of participation was
largely ineffable; the emotions it engendered were of the
kind which commonly enforced silence, not the demonstrative celebration urged by reformers. The Mass's meaning did
not depend on any specific function it had, whether understood in deeply theological or shallowly magical terms. Profoundly at home in the ritual, implicitly believing in its importance, worshipers might prefer a muted, silent celebration
of quiet affirmation. Anthropologists have noted that a strong
sense of the sacredness of ritual often manifests itself in ap-

parently routine behavior, an attitude of prudent participation but no visible deep emotion.[31]

As Clifford Geertz has summarized it, the function of sacred symbol is to synthesize a people's ethos—the tone, character, and quality of their life, their moral and esthetic style, mood, and world view, their most comprehensive idea of order. The ethos is shown to be eminently suitable to the actual state of reality.[32] Liturgical innovators contended that for Catholics the traditional symbols had ceased to perform these functions adequately, that there existed a deep split between the symbols and the actual conditions of modern life. Yet this was a split felt and perceived only by a relatively small segment of the Church, among them many whom Mary Douglas has described as being unattuned to symbolism in any form. If the radical critique of traditional liturgy was in part that this liturgy was no longer effective, in part it was also that this liturgy was too effective. It sustained a culture which the innovator wished to get beyond. It spoke of values he wished to discard. It was too God-centered, too sacred, too much oriented toward eternity. The widespread recognition of the irrelevance of the symbols did not occur until after they had been changed. The community whose symbols they were began to disintegrate only because the manipulation of the symbols itself promoted that disintegration. Especially deadly was the confusion sown, often deliberately, by the anointed guardians of the symbols—the priests who confessed their lack of belief in them or manipulated them for purposes alien to the traditions of the community. Of all the odd notions which accompanied the process of liturgical change, none was odder than the belief that a complex, dense, and ancient society which had built itself up laboriously through centuries of history could be destroyed and then rebuilt, according to plan, by experts.

Among unsophisticated people, however, Catholic folk religion has probably only rarely been mere "cultural Catholicism" in the sense of a system valued chiefly for its worldly benefits, its sense of belonging, with no real belief in God beyond it. Such a disjuncture of belief and action usually requires an element of sophistication which few "folk Catholics" possess. In however imperfect a way, the rites of folk Catholicism have kept alive a strong sense of divine reality. Studying the folk Catholicism of Spain, the anthropologist William A. Christian has noted that the dichotomy of sacred and profane is quite fundamental and that for some people it leads to a joyful and even poetic faith. A strong relationship with God can substitute for missing human relationships and helps the individual form his or her own identity, through interior dialogue with God. Newer forms of piety, propagated by young priests fresh from the seminaries, tend to obscure the sense that there exists "a world beyond the world." As Professor Christian has said, "By their hard-nosed rationalism the young priests live in a world where there is little or no participation of God in day-to-day affairs." He fears that the older religious culture will be effectively undermined before an equally powerful reformed piety can be forged.[33]

Although liturgical reform has brought about a theoretical improvement in the quality of Catholic piety, it is not at all clear that it has resulted in a stronger sense of God's presence in the Church, and there is a good deal of evidence to the contrary.

In the actual life of the Church, most sacred symbols are not understood by most believers in an explicit, intellectual way, but are nonetheless apprehended as having meaning.

The total effect of these symbols is to sustain a strong belief in God, even though specific symbols may not always convey specific religious meanings.

Despite their ignorance of the explicit meaning of particular symbols, uneducated Catholics tend to have a stronger loyalty to these symbols and to the traditions behind them than do the educated.

At certain periods of history the passive resistance of the uneducated to the process of symbolic manipulation is the major force tending toward the preservation of historical continuity in the Church.

Since public worship is the property of the total community of believers, liturgical specialists can claim only an advisory role in this area and should under certain circumstances give way to the authority of common practice.

Since the Catholic Church has throughout most of its history been composed largely of uneducated persons, the unity of the Church has been primarily in its worship rather than its belief. Folk Catholics have often been guilty of material heresy, as reformers charge, because the lack of adequate doctrinal grounding cannot help but lead to mistaken beliefs. But the material heresy of the uneducated has always been treated quite leniently, as being unintentional and unavoidable, while strong emphasis has been placed on conformity in ritual and worship, or at least on conformity in official liturgy with room for diversity in nonliturgical piety.

The primary unity of the Church is in its worship, in which a certain diversity of belief is possible so long as the liturgical unity is respected.

Unity in worship and diversity in belief can be maintained, however, only so long as doctrinal diversity does not become conscious opposition to the official teachings of the Church.

(That this is now coming to be the case is evidenced, for example, by the reluctance of some congregations to recite the Creed even when prescribed, or by changes in the prayers of the Mass evidently designed to imply heterodox beliefs.)

The Church of England and the Protestant Episcopal Church in the United States have for over a century tolerated within their borders far greater diversity of both belief and liturgy than has the Roman Catholic Church. The unity of these churches has been maintained primarily through the acceptance by all parties of a common Prayer Book, although this general acceptance has greatly weakened in recent years. In one sense the history of these two churches is evidence that there can be wide diversity within unity. In another sense, however, the diversity has been so great as to call into question how unified these churches really are. Extreme groups, both "high" and "low," have sometimes sought to read each other out of the Church. Anglo-Catholics may refuse to attend services in an Evangelical parish and vice versa. In America the very use of the term "Protestant" in the Church's official name has been periodically challenged as inappropriate by some groups, and just as vigorously defended by others. The unity of Anglicanism has sometimes seemed to be primarily an acceptance of the Church as a convenient and traditional administrative arrangement. Anglo-Catholics have commonly felt far closer to Roman Catholics and Eastern Orthodox than to Evangelical or "broad-church" Anglicans, and the latter two have often felt far greater affinity for various Protestant groups.

The same situation has begun to develop within Roman Catholicism, so that it is difficult to say that those who attend the Latin High Mass at Brompton Oratory in London, for example, belong to the same church as those gathered for the Eucharist in a student apartment in San Francisco. Their unity appears to be merely nominal, and quite often their attitudes toward each other do not seem to approach even respectful tolerance, much less anything greater.

Radical liturgical diversity in a church tends toward the decrease of both charity and unity.

The decline of the sacred within Catholicism has sometimes been attributed to the process of social change itself, which lies beyond the Church's own borders and largely beyond the control of its people. Mircea Eliade has theorized, for example, that urban man's religious sensibilities are weak and that in the modern milieu religion tends to become a largely private and greatly diluted phenomenon.[34] A. R. Radcliffe-Brown developed the thesis that religious cults and social structures decay together,[35] which has obvious applicability in an age when almost every institution in America, from the federal government to the family, appears to be in severe trouble. Social change has unquestionably affected the condition of popular religion. Traditional devotions, for example, fell into disuse not only because of liturgical reform but also because increasing crime and deteriorating public transportation made many people reluctant to attend church at night.

However, urban life is not of necessity the enemy of traditional religion. Robert Redfield found that in a city of Yucatán the purest kind of Catholicism was to be found, as well as the conscious preservation of rural pagan cults, both existing in the midst of a good deal of skepticism and indifference.[36] Mary Douglas, while noting that modern child-raising practices tend to create attitudes inimical to ritual, that education tends also to foster a certain religious skepticism, and that social change causes a decline of belief in ritual, also observes that secularism is not a distinctively modern phenomenon and is not confined to "advanced" societies. (Pygmies in Africa evince a "secular" or "skeptical" outlook, for example.)[37]

Perhaps the most impressive examples of the compatibility of sacred religion with both urban life and social change are to be found within American Catholicism itself, among the generations of immigrants from many countries who moved from the peasant villages of the Old World to the industrial cities of the New and found that in the process their religion was strengthened. No sense of dislocation experienced by their modern descendants is likely to be as great. (Mary Douglas makes a similar point about the Irish in London.) Paradoxically, it has not been the urban milieu which caused the weakening of American Catholicism. The enthusiasm of so many Catholics for Harvey Cox's original thesis about the essential secularity of the modern city is incomprehensible, since Catholics, of all people, should have been aware of quite strong religious traditions in the great cities of the United States. (Besides the urban Catholic parishes, the innumerable Negro storefront churches are obvious.)

The sudden weakening of American Catholicism in fact coincided with a massive Catholic abandonment of the city for the simulated small-town atmosphere of the suburbs. This process began immediately after World War II but reached its peak in the 1960s. So long as Catholics were city people their religious traditions were strong. The relationship of desacralization and suburbanization is complex, but in part both phenomena represent the desire on the part of Catholics to enter the mainstream of American life, to shed whatever identities are limiting and special. Within Anglicanism it is perhaps not accidental that the strongest ritualist parishes have more often been found in large cities than in small towns or rural communities.

The very conditions of urban life may tend to make city dwellers sensitive to tradition, religious ritual, and group religious identity.

That higher education tends to promote a certain skepticism about the sacred and about tradition is obvious, but the necessity of this is less certain. In its earlier stages the Liturgical Movement attracted most of its following from among educated people, who had been trained to appreciate the subtleties of a liturgy whose resources were not at all obvious. If a consciously modern liturgy is now largely the concern of the educated, it is also true that the restoration or purification of old liturgy has also been the concern of the educated. (Uneducated people tend to be conservatives but not reactionaries—they accept whatever is familiar to them.) The highly educated are if anything even more subject to fashion than the simple, and nothing is more likely than that before too many years there will be a revival of interest in traditional solemn liturgy among the educated, by which time many of the ordinary people in the parishes will have become used to the new ways and will regard the revival of the old with suspicion and incomprehension. (This happened in Anglicanism, where the common people were extremely slow to abandon their rituals in the sixteenth century but looked askance at the ritualist revival in the nineteenth.)

Folk religion, although it exists in many religions of the world, has not been a recognized part of most Protestant groups, including the Episcopal Church. One of the important distinguishing features of Protestantism has in fact been its refusal to sanction folk religion; this was one of the major issues of the Reformation. Thus the charge that contemporary Roman Catholicism is in danger of being protestantized is given added weight by the hostility of many reformers to the religious customs of their own people. Protestantism has no folk piety in that for the most part it does not sanction religious rites which are apart from the official worship and which express sensibilities different from what is expressed in the official worship. (Pietistic and Pentecostal sects may be exceptions to this.) Anglo-Catholics have perceived the importance of folk piety and have often sought to introduce it into their religious life. However, it functions there in a notably different way from its function in Roman Catholicism. In the latter it often has genuinely popular roots and is primarily used either by simple people or by sophisticated people who have imbibed it from childhood. In Anglo-Catholicism it tends to be the conscious adoption by sophisticated people of the piety of the simple. Anglo-Catholicism does not appear to have a "folk" constituency as Roman Catholicism does. Even successful ritualist slum priests most often convert the common people to their rites rather than building on existing customs.

NOTES

1. "Liturgy and Spiritual Personalism," *Worship*, XXXIV, 9 (October, 1960), p. 501.
2. Frederick McManus, "The Future: Its Hopes and Difficulties," in *The Revival of the Liturgy*, ed. McManus (New York, 1963), pp. 208, 211–12, 218.
3. Joseph M. Connolly, "The Renewal of the Church," in *The Renewal of Christian Education* (The Liturgical Conference, 1964), p. 7. The report of the Milwaukee quotation is by John Deedy, *Commonweal*, September 19, 1969, p. 554.
4. Mannion, "The Making of a Dissident," *Commonweal*, January 19, 1973, p. 344.
5. Gerard Sloyan, *Worship in a New Key: What the Council Teaches about Liturgy* (New York, 1965), pp. 16–17, 22–25, 68–69, 71, 139, 172–78. See also *Commonweal*, March 27, 1970, pp. 59–60.
6. Sövick, "Images of the Church," *Worship*, XLI, 3 (March, 1967), pp. 135–36.
7. Landon G. Dowdey, "Communities of Interest in the Modern City: a Challenge to Form New Kinds of Worship Groups," in O'Hanlon *et al.*, *Worship in the City of Man* (The Liturgical Conference, 1966), pp. 163, 167.
8. Robert Ledogar, M.M., "The Question of Daily Mass," *Worship*, XLIII, 5 (May, 1969), p. 258.
9. Richard Woods, O.P., *The Occult Revolution: a Christian Meditation* (New York, 1971), especially pp. 134, 141, 177–78, 215, 222–23, 225–28.

10. "Absurdity in Sacred Decoration," *Worship*, XXXIV, 5 (April, 1960), pp. 250, 252, 254–55.

11. "Gift for Father Godfrey Diekmann on His Jubilee as Editor of *Worship*," in *The Revival of the Liturgy*, p. 10.

12. Francis W. Mahoney, M.M., "The Aymara Indians: a Model for Liturgical Adaptation," *Worship*, XLV, 7 (August–September, 1971), p. 407.

13. "Liturgists, Biblicists in Liturgy Dispute," *The National Catholic Reporter*, May 12, 1972, pp. 1, 13. Also *ibid.*, June 23, 1972, pp. 8–9; June 9, 1972, p. 9.

14. Joseph T. Nolan in *The National Catholic Reporter*, February 25, 1972, p. 6.

15. *Natural Symbols*, pp. 7, 31, 42, 50.

16. *The Folk Culture of Yucatán* (Chicago, 1955), pp. 101–2, 256.

17. "Absurdity in Sacred Decoration," p. 255.

18. *Natural Symbols*, p. 42.

19. Michael M. Ames, "Buddha and the Dancing Goblins: a Theory of Magic and Religion," *American Anthropologist*, LXVI, 1 (February, 1964), pp. 75, 79. David G. Mandelbaum, "Transcendental and Pragmatic Religion," *ibid.*, LXVIII, 5 (October, 1966), pp. 1175–89.

20. *The Sacred and the Profane*, trans. Willard R. Trask (New York, 1959), pp. 122–23, 128.

21. *The Varieties of Religious Experience* (New York, 1957), p. 396.

22. See, for example, Felipe Berryman, "Popular Catholicism in Latin America," *Cross Currents*, XXI, 3 (Summer, 1971), pp. 284–301.

23. David F. Aberle, "Religio-Magical Phenomena and Power, Prediction, and Control," *Southwestern Journal of Anthropology*, XXII, 3 (Autumn, 1966), p. 222. Dorothy Hammond, "Magic: a Problem in Semantics," *American Anthropologist*, LXXII, 6 (December, 1970), pp. 1349–56. Murray and Rosalie Wax, "The Notion of Magic," with comments by various authors, *Current Anthropology*, IV, 5 (December, 1963), p. 504. William J. Goode, "Magic and Religion: a Continuum," *Ethnos*, XIV, 2–4 (April–December, 1949), pp. 172–82.

24. *Magic, Science, and Religion* (Garden City, N.Y., 1955), pp. 17–18, 28–29.

25. Redfield, *The Folk Culture of Yucatán*, p. 326. Keith Thomas, *Religion and the Decline of Magic* (New York, 1971), pp. 238, 264–65, 277.

26. Roland Mayer, S.M., "On Witchcraft," *St. Louis Review*, October 22, 1971, p. 12.

27. *Elementary Forms*, p. 403.

28. James W. Fernandez, "Symbolic Consensus in a Fang Reformation Cult," *American Anthropologist*, LXVII, 4 (August, 1965), pp. 906–8.

29. "Myths and Rituals: a General Theory," *Reader in Comparative Religion*, ed. Lessa and Vogt (New York, 1965), pp. 145–58.

30. Fernandez, "Symbolic Consensus," p. 925.

31. Durkheim, *Elementary Forms*, p. 41. Redfield, *The Folk Culture of Yucatán*, p. 311.

32. "Religion as a Cultural System," *The Religious Situation: 1968*, ed. Donald R. Cutler (Boston, 1968), pp. 641–42.

33. *Person and God in a Spanish Valley* (New York, 1972), pp. 161, 178, 184–87. See also Allen Spitzer, "Aspects of Religious Life in Tepoztan," *Anthropological Quarterly*, XXX, 1 (January, 1957), pp. 1–17; "Notes on Merida Parish," *ibid.*, XXXI, 1 (January, 1958), pp. 3–20.

34. *The Sacred and the Profane*, pp. 178–79.

35. *Structure and Function in Primitive Society* (Glencoe, Ill., 1952), p. 164.

36. *The Folk Culture of Yucatán*, pp. 110, 235.

37. *Natural Symbols*, pp. ix–x, 5–6, 144.

CHAPTER 7

The Reformed Liturgy

The official Roman Catholic liturgical changes implemented after the Second Vatican Council, and the proposed changes in Episcopalian worship contained in the *Services for Trial Use*, were not for the most part intended to be radical, although in certain ways they did mark momentous departures from traditional practice, especially in the official language. In the light of unauthorized liturgical practices in the past decade, or of the most advanced liturgical thought, they must be considered relatively conservative, with the exception of the Episcopalian third eucharistic service, which encourages free improvisation and, if given final approval, will probably be adopted by some congregations as their usual celebration, despite its not being authorized for that.

The severe problems created by free liturgical experimentation do not therefore apply of necessity to the new official rites, which were clearly devised to maintain continuity with the traditions of the past and, most important, to provide norms of liturgical uniformity and stability.

At the same time, these official changes have been of such magnitude (even if dismissed by radicals as timid) as to have caused severe disturbance to many people. The fact that such changes have been authorized by the highest governing bodies of the respective churches has lent support to those who charge that the old rituals are irrelevant; hence the new official liturgies inevitably invite the criticism of not going far enough, of maintaining a timid compromise position. The fact of conspicuous liturgical change under official sanction helps create an atmosphere in which unauthorized changes are more readily dared, in which liturgical stability is undermined, and in which symbolically it is declared that a new era has been inaugurated. (Thus some advanced liturgists can accuse the Roman Church of failing to carry out the spirit of the Vatican Council, despite that body's demonstrable caution in liturgical matters.) Once striking official changes have been mandated, this is taken by many people as a signal for general revolution.

The cause of legitimate liturgical change has been harmed by the sense which many people have that some liturgists do in fact regard it as only the beginning. Many of those most active in winning the official changes subsequently expressed their disappointment at the relative conservatism of the reforms. It became a commonplace in liturgical circles to predict that more radical changes would have to come. Many liturgists justified unauthorized experiments, and obviously came to regard the Church's official pronouncements as at best general guidelines which could be disregarded. (The editor of *Worship*, for example, hoped for "extremely free adaptations" of the Latin texts into English.[1]) The difference between "moderate" and "radical" liturgists has sometimes seemed mainly a matter of timing and strategy rather than of substance; few moderates have opposed radical experimentation with any apparent urgency.

Virtually all liturgists seem to have greatly underestimated the effects of liturgical change even when carried out with official sanction. Almost no one appears to have foreseen the antagonism, the schisms, the confusion, the dissatisfactions on both the right and the left which followed. Few strategies were devised for coping with the confusions, alienations, and uncertainties which ritual change occasioned, and the strategies which were employed tended to exacerbate the problem. Many liturgists appeared surprised that there was no relatively painless and efficient transition from the old ways to the new.

Apart from the merits of the various specific changes, change itself was a principal cause of anxiety and dislocation in the Church. In retrospect it is easy to see what was not perceived at the time—that no conservative body with an ancient and sacred system of symbols can alter these significantly without a severe spiritual crisis occurring, which for many people will be a fundamental crisis of personal identity. The liturgists' bias toward explicit meanings contributed to this, in that it was assumed that once the rationale for the various changes was explained, they would be readily accepted. The fact that for most people the symbols held implicit meanings which were even more important than the explicit ones was largely overlooked. Speaking of the introduction of the English liturgy by the Anglican Church in the sixteenth century, the historian A. L. Rowse has said:

. . . we shall see operating, as the result of the Reformation, a kind of rationalizing campaign on the part of the Reformers and Puritans against the proliferations of the unconscious, the superfluities and elaborations of belief. . . . No doubt it meant some progress in rationalization; at the same time it involved a certain impoverishment of the life of the unconscious, deliberate restrictions upon its free movement, in part direction in accordance with the (not wholly) rational will.[2]

It is difficult for anyone without a knowledge of anthropology to appreciate fully the astonishing audacity, the profound disturbance to the unconscious levels upon which a society lives its life, of such an action as the substitution of an English liturgy for the age-long Latin rite of Western Christendom in which Englishmen had been swaddled time out of mind . . . nothing can detract from the revolutionary audacity of such an interference with the customary, the subconscious, the ritual element in life.[3]

Rather ominously, the easy acceptance of liturgical change was made to seem dependent on people's not taking the symbols too seriously, on their being able to shed one set and put on another almost like changing their clothes for a new season. Oddly, in an age when freedom was being reemphasized in the Church, the acceptance of liturgical change was made into a great act of obedience; many people who prided themselves on their loyalty to the hierarchy now consciously put aside their doubts and personal misgivings to fall in line with the new ritual. Those for whom the symbols had the deepest meaning were often among those who suffered the greatest anxieties, precisely for that reason.

Sacred rituals cannot be reformed substantially without serious dislocation in the society whose symbols they are.
Those for whom traditional symbols have the deepest meaning tend to be those most affected by change. This can take the form either of liturgical conservatism, as the individual perceives that the alteration of the symbols will have profound effects on the lives of those concerned, or of liturgical radicalism stemming from the same perception.

That liturgical change did not have even more profound effects is mainly owing to the prevailing pragmatic spirit which enables people to keep symbols from being too much a part of their lives; it is the facility which allows modern man to live much of his life at the surface level and not become deeply attached to very many things.

The almost universal crisis of the spirit through which Roman Catholics passed after the Council had many causes, but one of the most important was the simple fact of liturgical turmoil and instability itself. Although liturgists quickly developed the position that modern man ought to learn to pray in an atmosphere of distraction and worldly pressure, most people seem to want islands of quiet and recollection in their lives. (It is in any case not clear that the hubbub of modern life is any greater than in the cities and castles of the past.) The process of liturgical change was handled badly from a number of points of view: the people were never consulted as to their wants and needs; there was insufficient education in the new ways prior to their introduction; change was often presented as a hierarchical command to be obeyed; there were conflicting signals about the rationale for the changes (for example, was it to restore the ancient liturgy or to come to terms with modern culture?); change was piecemeal and hence doubly confusing. Although many liturgists oppose it, a permanent missal for the laity would be an important symbol at this time, implying that a new age of stability has been reached. The present welter of discardable booklets, mimeographed sheets, divergent paperback hymnals, etc. is not only confusing but appears to signify a haphazard, impermanent, jerry-built liturgy and has unfortunate psychological effects. Habits of irreverence and inattention are built up, for example, by the feeling that rites currently being used may be revised or discarded and hence are of little significance.

An atmosphere of liturgical disorder and instability is likely to cause a diminution of the spirit of prayer.

The process of liturgical change in the Episcopal Church, possibly deriving from its relatively decentralized structure and possibly also from an observance of the unfortunate experiences of the Roman Church, has been better planned. No sharp break with the past is required because the traditional Prayer Book has not been outlawed and the first eucharistic service in the trial Prayer Book is in any case similar to the traditional service. The proposed changes have been presented altogether and at one time, so they can be experienced and evaluated as a whole. Priests and laity have been given ample opportunity to try the proposals and record their impressions. The strongly negative reactions from many people probably ensure at a minimum that no one will be forced to accept liturgical changes unwillingly.

Of their very nature, liturgical changes cannot be evaluated adequately in a brief period of time. Hence an overall assessment of the wisdom of the Roman Church's action must wait some years, until the long-term effects can be discerned. Among the questions which will have to be asked are whether the Church's quantitative decline is in fact matched by a qualitative growth, whether the evident trend toward secularization reverses itself, whether new and enduring forms of popular devotion develop, and whether the new liturgy becomes as deeply ingrained in the life of the people as the old was. In the meantime, however, certain tentative judgments can be made.

For all its tendency to become a shibboleth, the greatest gain in the process of reform has been the attainment of a decent level of participation by the laity, a level which will probably improve over the years. Provided it is not simply entered into as a duty, and provided the entire Mass is not taken up with unison prayers and songs so as to prevent private prayer and silence, the custom of prayer and song in common can only add to the solemnity and meaningfulness of the service. Catholicism tends to favor the external expression of interior states, and the wholly silent Mass was always to some extent an anomaly. The habit of communal prayer and song also tends to ingrain these in people's consciousness, a strategy for devotion which the Church has persistently recognized.

Since Catholicism tends to favor the external expression of internal states, communal participation in liturgy is more authentically Catholic than silent participation. It is also expressive of the Catholic spirit of communalism, in which worship is the act of the whole Church.

Liturgical change has also brought clear advantages insofar as it has restored or reemphasized certain symbols which had been lost or obscured. The restored Easter Vigil, which, however, predated the Second Vatican Council by some years, is the most important of these. The new place of Baptism—conferred in the body of the church, often in public and in conjunction with the Eucharist, is another. So are the Offertory procession, the Acclamations following the consecration, and the foot-washings on Holy Thursday. To some degree the effectiveness of the central liturgical symbols has been increased by clearing away many of the decorative objects which Thomas Merton and others had complained of. Up to a point the penchant for liturgical and artistic simplification has been a healthy influence.

The vernacular has on the whole been a positive change, the best evidence of which is in the fact that most lay people probably now prefer it to the Latin. It makes participation possible on still another level beyond the unison recitation or singing of Latin, although the latter is not to be too easily dismissed. The vernacular is, however, a mixed blessing. It does tend to detract from the mystery of the rite. This is not simply because the Latin was shallow and theatrical obfuscation. Rather, the use of Latin conveyed a sense of timelessness and ancient tradition, which is so important to the experience of the sacred. It also reminded worshipers that the mystery in which they participated was finally unutterable in comprehensible language. The old ritual conveyed the sense that much more was happening than met the eye; the new asks to be accepted purely in its own terms.

The Latin is also so close to the Church's liturgical and theological wellsprings that its abandonment has left many people badly out of touch with their traditions. Its demise has been one of the principal stimuli to the belief that liturgy ought to be a completely contemporary thing. Ways must be found of preserving some element of Latin as part of the Church's living worship.

The association of the Latin language with the timeless, mysterious, and traditional aspects of worship is so profound that no fully adequate translation of it into the vernacular is possible.

The decision to translate the liturgy into the vernacular has had momentous consequences which should not be minimized. It may lead to the disappearance of almost all sense of the sacred in liturgy except among people who feed upon their earlier formation in the old rites. It may lead to a new and greatly revitalized way of apprehending the sacred. In certain ways it may be the most important change authorized by the Second Vatican Council. Unfortunately, few liturgists perceived its significance at the time; a vernacular liturgy was urged for the sake of "better understanding," as though it were merely the equivalent of installing new microphones in the churches or persuading the priests to speak more distinctly.

A decline of a sense of the sacred was inevitably fostered by the very fact of liturgical change, especially since the antiquity of the old rites had been exaggerated and people had been allowed to assume that the liturgy would never change. Mary Douglas has pointed out that belief in ritual tends to decline as it is discovered to what degree persons manipulate it.[4] This was revealed quite publicly and deliberately at the Second Vatican Council and by the rather in-

eptly handled alterations which followed. It was intensified
was intended deliberately to demythologize the ritual. Peter
Berger claims that religion tends to conceal how much of
by widespread liturgical experimentation, some of which
the sacred is man-made, so that the periodic revelation of
this fact has momentous consequences.[5] Clifford Geertz as-
serts that one of the purposes of ritual is to portray human
choices as though imposed.[6] The conservative function of
ritual is thus revealed, and a ritualistic religion can be merely
a prop for an oppressive society. However, precisely because
of its "irrelevance" it need have no close ties to the political
order at all, which has enabled devout Catholics to espouse
all shades of political opinion. (That the avoidance of ritual
in religion is no protection from political conservatism was
illustrated by the election of a Quaker president in 1968.)
Moreover, the fragility of meaning in human relationships is
such that it is a mistake to dismiss the sacred character of
ritual as merely a man-made illusion. Viewed from a certain
perspective, all things human—love and marriage, political
loyalty, art—are "merely" man-made and in some sense illusory. Yet the belief that they are also more than human,
more than illusory, is central to their significance and ultimately more "true" than the bald facts about their origins.

*Rapid and visible transformation of ritual has the effect
of desacralizing it.*

*The concept of "experimental liturgy" is contradictory and
self-defeating if liturgy is to be sacral, because the spirit of
experimentation, implying detachment, criticism, and conscious manipulation, is incompatible with the spirit of reverence and humility required by sacral rites.*

The new Roman liturgy seems deficient also in certain
details of its reformation, erring principally on the side of ill-

conceived and unnecessary simplifications. A decided puritanical bias is detectible throughout, which has had unfortunate effects. A few examples:

Entrance Rite: In many parishes this is perfunctory and undramatic. The elimination of the old prayers at the foot of the altar greatly weakens the sense that the priest is about to enter a holy place, before which he has paused to prepare himself. It is worth noting that the beautiful Psalm 42 was regarded by Josef Jungmann as highly appropriate for the entrance ceremony.[7]

Confiteor: The truncation of this prayer was unnecessary, especially the elimination of the saints formerly invoked. The sense of remembrance of great saints from the past is an important part of traditional liturgy. Most unfortunate was the reduction of the triple recitation "through my fault, through my fault, through my most grievous fault" to a single staid acknowledgment. This was one of the most familiar, almost archetypal, moments of the entire Mass, and in the Latin it had become virtually a proverb. An important opportunity to maintain continuity was lost. The psychological effect of the triple recitation was overlooked, and the result is flat and pedestrian.

Responsorial Psalm: Partly because of quite undistinguished translations, this also is flat and mechanical. As a form of congregational participation it often seems like a duty rather than a willing prayer. Some kind of singing might be preferable.

Washing of the Priest's Hands: The elimination of Psalm 25 in favor of a mere few words seems pointless and takes away a moving and appropriate scriptural passage, as well as one of great familiarity.

Canon: The elimination of almost all saints' names from three of the four eucharistic prayers (in the first, most of them are merely optional) again weakens the sense of historical continuity. These prayers might have been revised to include more familiar saints than the Roman martyrs previously remembered, and this could have been an effective expression of the Church's continuous unfolding through time.

Communion: The simple statement "the Body of Christ" is to the point but also lends itself to a rushed, mechanical repetition by the priest. The old formula was particularly beautiful. "May the Body of Our Lord Jesus Christ preserve your soul into everlasting life."

Announcements: As presently situated, they convey the impression that they are what the Church most wants the faithful to remember as they depart from the liturgy. They are ridiculously anticlimactic and should be restored to their old place before the homily or perhaps put before the beginning of the Mass.

Altogether the language of the reformed Mass is, at best, undistinguished. It is modern but in the same way that a newspaper article or directions for assembling a mechanical object are modern. Almost nothing about it is memorable, powerful, or poetic. As Ralph Keifer, the secretary of the International Committee on English in the Liturgy, has said:

If anything is wrong with the language of the new eucharistic prayers, it is precisely the attempt at modernity. The curious editing of the ancient sources has left us with feeble and hackneyed versions of the more powerful originals.[8]

Most worshipers are probably not consciously sensitive to the literary qualities of the Mass prayers, but it is in the nature of symbolism, including language, that it has effects on people in ways they do not realize. It is doubtful if anything in the present English text will ever become as ingrained in people's minds as the *"mea culpa, mea culpa, mea maxima culpa,"* the *"Dominus vobiscum,"* or the *"Domine non sum dignus"* of the old rite. It is also highly ironic that, even as liturgists insist dogmatically on the need to pray in the vernacular, people are required to address God by the unfamiliar and rather grating, even if philologically correct, "Yahweh." Although an excellent translation probably could not have been prepared within the brief time available for the introduction of the vernacular, it surely remains a crucial need for the future.

As serious as the poverty of language in the new English liturgy, and obviously related to it, is the poverty of gesture, which seems to be the result of the same misguided puritan spirit. There are few good reasons, for example, to have eliminated the genuflection during the Creed, the frequent signs of the cross, the ringing of bells, and in many parishes the use of incense except at funerals and during Holy Week. Liturgical reformers dismissed these as "decadent" historical accretions,[9] but they were an intimate part of traditional public worship and it is not at all evident that their abolition has improved the quality of the service, except perhaps for those who have in mind some abstract notion of what a correct Eucharist might be like.

The official elimination of some familiar gestures has caused others to fall into disuse through the apparent belief that they too have been suppressed, or a general confusion as to what is or is not now prescribed. Included are the crosses traced on forehead, lips, and heart before the Gospel, striking the breast during the *Confiteor,* and the sign of the cross after receiving Communion. In some churches kneeling has fallen into disuse altogether, and there are even remodeled chapels where the benches have been set so close together that kneeling is made impossible. The claim that standing is appropriate to the Mass because it is the "Resurrection position" ignores the popular tradition about kneeling—it is not commonly regarded as a mark of penitence but of deep reverence, and especially as a sign of respect for the Real Presence. Other unnecessary and ill-advised diminutions of ritual include the drastic truncation of the Holy Thursday procession, always a major expression of popular devotion to the Eucharist, and the elimination of the *Asperges* or the *Vidi Aquam*, both quite beautiful uses of Psalms 50 and 117, before High Mass. The suppression of *Tenebrae* in Holy Week, apparently on what is the merely technical grounds that the next day's Office should not be anticipated, and the reduction of the ceremony of the stripping of the altar to merely a private one on Holy Thursday, are other examples of changes which may satisfy some strict and rather arcane liturgical principle but merely weaken the symbolic power of the ceremonies. It is symptomatic of the present confused state of liturgy that few people seem entirely sure which traditional ceremonies are still in effect and which are not. It is a confusion which appears to extend even to many of the clergy. (There is a common misimpression, which in some cases has been propagated by liturgists, that the Mass may no longer be said in Latin at all.)

Before the Council, Thomas Merton had expressed a common viewpoint within the Liturgical Movement when he argued that modern man has a diminished sensitivity to symbol, which is indicated among other ways by a taste for what is merely decorative.[10] The importance of gesture was then recognized, as for example by one prominent liturgist who said that "even in the liturgical rite most in need of radical change, the smallest measure of outward participation represents some inner activity." [11]

Oddly, however, as reform proceeded, and despite the fact that some advanced liturgists want even to introduce new actions like dancing into worship, gestures were more and more pruned and simplified, often with no evident good reason and often also in ways open to misinterpretation (for example, the disuse of kneeling as possibly signifying lack of belief in the Real Presence). It became obvious that reformers wished to place primary emphasis on the words of the

rite, uninspiring though they are, and seemed to regard gestures as rather superfluous and distracting. The result has
been a liturgy which is undramatic and wordy, in which
worshipers, except for standing, sitting, and kneeling, have
little to do and are mainly supposed to develop their powers
of concentration so as to get maximum benefit from the
words being read. It is a kind of puritanism which failed to
note that historically Catholics associate this kind of worship with Protestantism and that Catholicism has through
most of its history favored a worship rich in gesture. Cardi-
nal Newman, for example, thought gestures alone—the lay-
ing on of hands, the pouring of water, etc.—would be sufficient to convey the meaning of the sacraments even without
words.[12] The suppression of familiar traditional gestures has
predictably given rise to proposals that new gestures like
dancing be introduced, since "Faith . . . is a disposition
towards God which is actualized only in expression. . . . So
no faith exists that is not actualized in a rite, that is, indis-
solubly efficacious gesture and word." [13] An important principle is in danger of being lost:

*Catholicism tends to worship God in gesture as much as in
word—unlike Protestantism, which is preeminently a religion of the Word. The cult of spontaneity necessarily inhibits this, since it regards ritualized gesture as merely external.*

The proposed liturgical changes in the Episcopal Church
appear to suffer from similar deficiencies, although on the
whole the English of the second eucharistic service, even if
not of the highest quality, is better than that authorized for
the Roman Catholic Church in America. The proposal to
abandon the Book of Common Prayer as the uniform liturgy
of the Episcopal Church is especially fraught with consequences because the familiar and powerful words of the
Prayer Book have been the basic focus of unity in what is

otherwise a liturgically and theologically quite diverse church. Those who fear the loss of the great classic texts of the Prayer Book—the Collect for Purity, the General Confessions and Absolutions at Morning Prayer and in the Eucharist, and the Prayer of Humble Access—are not necessarily being nostalgic. They recognize that these words have a proven power to move people deeply, something which the new and more pedestrian words do not. If a prayer is memorable its effectiveness is greatly extended, since it can work in people's minds even outside the times of formal devotion. The Prayer Book sentences have a powerful rhythm built into them which helps to make them a part of people's basic consciousness. Little in the new liturgies gives sign of being particularly memorable. Advanced Anglo-Catholic liturgists also appear to have a bias against traditional gestures.

The effectiveness of new liturgies has sometimes been established simply by fiat, in apparent accord with the principle that whatever has been done for the sake of reform must be good. Thus a prominent Roman Catholic theologian can say with assurance:

The adult Catholic who goes to church on Sunday morning finds that the change has made the liturgy a very beautiful, simple, understandable, and moving ritual. The symbolism, once covered over with too much paint, has become clear again. The message of the Mass is clearly cast into the very form of celebration.

(Revealing the pervasive contempt which professionals have for the rank and file, he has also said that while the distinction between sacred and profane was widely accepted in the Church, it was never accepted by theologians, who can now disabuse the people of their mistaken ideas.)[14] When a distinguished international group, including Joan Sutherland, Yehudi Menuhin, C. Day Lewis, and Graham Greene, protested on esthetic grounds the suppression of the Mass of

Pius V, various English clergy presumed to inform them that
they had been mistaken, that there was little of esthetic
value in the traditional rite. One monsignor said the old
Mass might be permitted for use by elderly people within
five or ten years.[15] (One of the less convincing aspects of the
claim that Roman Catholic liturgical reform has succeeded
is the liturgists' reluctance to allow the new rite to compete
on its merits with the old. Where such competition has been
allowed during the trial period of the new liturgy in the
Episcopal Church, popular support for the new has not been
nearly sufficient to permit it to displace the old.)

The new Roman liturgy has achieved general acceptance,
and a majority of worshipers would probably not want to
return to the Latin. At the same time there is little enthusiasm for the new rite, and no one has said it is beautiful or
memorable. It has not inspired the deep attachment which
many people had for the Latin. Declining church attendance,
while not necessarily attributable to the new liturgy, nonetheless casts a pall over any claims of general success. Even
more serious is the widespread dissatisfaction with the new
rite on the part of those who were in the forefront of the
struggle to get it adopted but who now feel the necessity of
constructing their own rites. What has been achieved is a
political solution—extremists have been cut off at both ends,
and those in the middle have accepted a compromise.

Ralph Keifer points out that in the old liturgy, although
Roman Catholics were often described as inert and passive:

even the very clerical and sober rite of low mass carried with it a
sense of involvement, by silent attentions, bows, kneeling, cross-
ings, breast-beating, and attention to "Mass devotions."

The new rites were supposed to have restored active participation in the liturgy and a more balanced sense of the paschal mystery. It is doubtful if we have restored either; we have probably,
in many cases, stamped out the last vestiges of both. A vivid and

concrete appreciation of the incarnation and the atonement has . . . often been bleached into vague shibboleths about "community" and "joy" and "peace" and "love". . . . The dropping of the old passion pieties . . . has not meant a renewed appreciation of the presence of the risen and exalted Lord; it has meant simply that Jesus becomes a vague teacher from the past. Instead of a deeper sense of participation, people feel less engaged than before and complain of a loss of a sense of "mystery." The young frankly admit they are bored. . . .

For a church which prides itself on being sacramental, we have little to give people the sense of presence and engagement that touch, taste, and smell bring to worship . . . kneeling, signs of the cross, beating of the breast, and bows recede more and more into the past . . . an intellectualized liturgy discourages "primitive" gestures. . . .

Such unrelenting wordiness is indeed both dull and puritan in the extreme. Nor is it surprising that people complain that the "new mass" lacks poetry and a sense of mystery. Unrelieved chatter, however exalted, is inimical to both.

. . . theologians are priding themselves on more successful communication than they actually enjoy if they think they have permitted a new theological consciousness among devout laity. The only significant act of communication has been ritual; if the old devotions have become "irrelevant," it is because our pseudo-patristic and highly verbal liturgy has rendered them so.[16]

The Episcopalian liturgist Daniel Stevick has pointed out the dilemma of the liturgical reformer: the choice between a very powerful but traditional idiom of worship and an idiom which is modern but also weak and unimpressive. He cites the literary critic Dwight Macdonald's comments on the Revised Standard Version of the Bible: "To make . . . readable in the modern sense means to flatten out, tone down, and convert into tepid expository prose. . . . It means stepping down the voltage . . . so it won't blow any fuses." [17] The Catholic philosopher Michael Novak has said bluntly that

There is no death any longer in the Mass. No irony. No bite. The Mass was not translated into English, it was translated into optimism and suburban cheer. The meaning of the Mass was never joy, peace, or celebration, or festivity—not in some direct recognition, not by some Rotarian enthusiasm. . . .[18]

Daniel Stevick's solution to the dilemma is to choose a fully modern idiom which can perhaps be powerful and compelling because it makes no compromises with the old. It is in fact one of the curiosities of the new liturgies that they accept as "modern" what is merely the presently fashionable outpourings of popular culture. It is probably not true that modern culture is incapable of creating a truly sacred idiom. Until liturgists became enamored of secularity, some very powerful and impressive modern churches were being built and religious art in general appeared to be in a flourishing state. There is an extensive repertoire of modern sacred music, of which Stravinsky's works are not by any means the only representatives. Yet rarely is such music heard in worship. The problem is partly practical, in that modern music is generally difficult and requires trained musicians and singers. But it appears to be also a matter of taste. Liturgical reformers have in many cases lent their authority to the teenage idiom of guitars and "folk" music, and decreed that this is to be modern man at worship. Strangely, modernizers have been among these fostering the impression that it is necessary to choose between Ray Repp on the one hand, and Gregorian Chant or the old Marian hymns on the other.

Truly modern styles of artistic worship—in music, in poetry, to a great extent in painting—would fail to jibe with fashionable liturgical ideas precisely for the reason indicated by Michael Novak—they are unsuitable to a worship seeking to build itself on shallow and sentimental notions of "love" and "community." The superficiality of so much pop music fits in well with the superficiality of present notions of what worship is supposed to be: the artificial stimulation of a fragile and ephemeral sense of community such as experienced at a rock concert. The new liturgy no longer has any room for the *Dies Irae*, and modernists often express discomfort at having to say the *Gloria*. The *Exultet* is no very important prayer for people with little need to be saved. Instead the new liturgy seems to aim at a safe and moderate range of human experience. Christians are not to be very conscious of their sins, and hence not very conscious either of the meaning of redemption. A warm sense of community is to blanket everything, obliterating peaks and valleys, lulling those who may be tempted to lift up their eyes or cast them down.

The new style of liturgy is greatly popular in high schools and colleges, where it is tied closely to the ephemera of the youth culture and to youth's sense of special identity. It does not appear capable of nourishing in most students a deep commitment to or involvement in the Church's worship, as evidenced in the reports that students rarely attend church when they are away from their special campus liturgies. Such liturgies partly succeed through their strong sense of alienation from the larger world of adults.

There is some evidence, however, that the new liturgy is also gaining in popularity in those places supposed to be the bastions of a sterile conservatism—the suburbs, at least among the younger middle class. That this should be the case is not surprising, because unintentionally the new liturgy seems designed to fit the new middle-class culture. It eschews formality, solemnity, and complexity in favor of a casual and utilitarian style. Years ago William Whyte noticed in *The Organization Man* the tendency of many suburbanites to prefer nondogmatic, ethically oriented, community-service churches, and this trend has finally come to be felt within Catholicism. Worshipers can now hear in church words not greatly different in tone from those television commentators use. The music is similar to what is played at pop concerts. Archaic symbols have been all but eliminated from the ritual. Everything is quite consciously "modern," and new techniques are tried out with regularity. There is now a generation of people who have to a great extent given up their traditions and willingly adopted a mobile style of life in which everything is newly minted, progress is taken for granted, and the past is something boring and unpleasant.

The affirmative secularity and community-mindedness of the new liturgy corresponds to similar attitudes in many such people, who are not in any serious way estranged from contemporary society, at least not at the conscious level. At present, where such people do not find a sufficiently modern liturgy in their parishes, they frequently go elsewhere— to a college chapel, for example. The decline of the practice of confession occurs in a milieu which advocates "self-fulfill-ment" as a primary duty and is increasingly reluctant to accept limitations of any kind. A religion which speaks of the "other-world" may seem irrelevant to people who find this life basically rewarding and who have accepted a sophisticated version of the idea of instantaneous gratification. On the other hand, those least at home in the new liturgy appear to be the mostly older people who are left behind in the crumbling cities, see little which is hopeful or gratifying in the present life, and are perhaps more disposed to reflect on eternity. In ten years' time the strongest support for the newer modes of worship will probably be amid the suburban middle class, while the self-consciously radical, the seminarians, and the college students will be searching for a resacralized idiom.

Daniel Stevick has pointed out several major advantages of a fixed and traditional rite, namely, that it saves the Church from having to create and discard new liturgies continually as theological and liturgical schools succeed each other in dominance, and it forces each school to modify its one-sidedness in order to fit in with the whole church.[19] Reformers have now succeeded in creating a liturgy which is modestly successful in relating to certain groups of people alive at the present time (although this relevance is often achieved only by going beyond what is officially permitted in the new liturgy). However, whether this same idiom will seem meaningful ten years from now, in an age when tastes and styles change rapidly, is doubtful. Already the swing back from "secularity" to a "fantasy" has made the new liturgy look bare and puritan. A generation of young Catholics is growing up with almost no experience of the traditional sacral mode of worship. Inevitably people's horizons tend to be limited by what they have experience of. Catholics of the future, while perhaps vaguely dissatisfied with their utilitarian style of worship, may have no real knowledge of the possibility of the sacred and may have to go to other traditions like the Eastern Orthodox to find it.

Similar problems exist with respect to the Episcopal liturgy, principally in regard to language. The liturgist Charles D. Keyes has asked, "Does the flattening out of the sense of finitude and the sublime in LLS [trial liturgy] really do justice to man's actual situation and his most profound needs?" And he adds:

The new iconoclasm is no longer puritanically offended by small things like candles and vestments. Instead, it is an iconoclasm about big things, namely the basic symbols of transcendence or whatever wakes a sense of awe before the sublime. Indeed the symbols of transcendence aren't *useful* either in jacking up a crumbling establishment or for copying on political placards. Still the peculiar fact remains that without them man loses his dignity. The attempt to reduce life and religion to common sense terms of reference is a self-defeating process.[20]

There is a notable inconsistency between the broad and eclectic humanism which advanced liturgists profess and their puritanism toward the worshiping traditions of their own churches. At the least, even if religious ritual is seen as purely a human creation, it should be respected as among the most important of such creations. Catholicism has of course always insisted that it is much more than that. There is at present an unhappy schizophrenia in liturgy, marked, on the one hand, by an official ritual which has been flattened out and drastically simplified and, on the other, by an eagerness to try new things so long as they appear lively and contemporary. The two poles, often adhered to by the same people, represent the influence of Protestant theology on the first side, with its severe and systematic attack on the sacred, and the influence of the counter-culture, the desire to keep abreast of modern developments, on the other. In the middle, traditional rich Catholic liturgy tends to get squeezed out.

Mary Douglas has noticed that loosened social bonds tend to stimulate effervescent religious expression. However, as millenarians throw away the old symbols, they also discover that communal life is rendered difficult precisely because of this. Hence the search for new symbols begins, a search which is obstructed by ingrained habits of iconoclasm in the rebels. Where visible symbols have been discarded as rigid and idolatrous, equally rigid if less tangible symbols may replace them, such as a fundamentalist attitude toward the Bible.[21] The often desperate struggle for "meaningful" liturgy has been made necessary precisely because existing symbols and rituals were discarded or altered drastically. Liturgical eclecticism has been the result of this, as dissatisfied worshipers ransack the various religious traditions of the world for usable symbols with which to replace their own. The new fundamentalism has appeared in a variety of guises —magic, the Jesus Movement, rigid ideological politics, neo-

Pentecostalism. Liturgists were drawn in theory to a puritan idea of worship. In practice, however, it has proved unsatisfying and has given rise to all manner of extravagant emotionalism. The suppression of the imagination in worship has given play to many ungoverned religious fantasies. Whatever may be said about the Pentecostal movement, it is doubtful that it would have gained so much strength in Catholicism if so many traditional devotional outlets had not been systematically closed. A religion richer in folk piety than perhaps any in the world has been reduced to borrowing its most notable contemporary folk idiom from fundamentalist Protestants, a fact which in itself strongly suggests that something is drastically wrong with the renewal of prayer life in the Church.

Catholicism generally prefers what is rich and complex to what is simple and direct. The attempt to reduce the former to the latter produces severe dislocations in the system, which tend to thwart the attempt at simplicity.

An illustration of this principle is perhaps found in the adoption of the new funeral liturgy, which is dominated by the affirmation of the Resurrection and which has expunged almost all expression of dread or sorrow. Yet this new rite has been introduced almost precisely at the moment when a strong faith in life after death is more in question among Catholics than ever before. When the official funeral liturgy expressed many thoughts of fear and sadness, most Catholics probably believed implicitly in resurrection; now that it affirms resurrection (and in the process has given up one of its most powerful and impressive rituals) many people find it harder to believe in that possibility.

The desacralization of liturgy has been principally due to the interpretations put on liturgical change by innovators acting without official sanction. However, it is also necessary to inquire to what extent the official changes themselves have contributed to that result, perhaps contrary to intention. Victor Turner, for example, believes the changes were motivated by questionable behavioral and materialist assumptions about ritual, especially the belief that it is supposed to reflect the social structure in which it operates. He also thinks the unspoken needs of the majority of believers, especially the need for interior prayer, were ignored by reformers.[22] A Dutch professor rejoices that the new liturgy deliberately desacralizes the rite and makes few concessions to traditionalists.[23] Daniel Stevick argues for revision of the Episcopal liturgy on the grounds that it is now harder to make statements about God than it once was, and in any case statements about God are perhaps really statements about man.[24] An Anglican liturgist has argued for the revision of the Prayer Book not, as is usually claimed, because it fails to speak to modern man but because it speaks all too effectively, proclaiming a transcendent God instead of the worldly faith now required.[25]

A liturgical idiom which powerfuly conveys a sense of the sacred in modern form is perhaps possible, despite Charles Davis's doubts. However, such an idiom has not as yet been created, and each new modern liturgy which appears seems merely to reduce the feeling for the sacred even more, sometimes by intention, sometimes through ineptness. If traditional liturgy conveys a sense of the sacred better than modern forms, that is all the more reason for keeping it, since it gives to this age something it would otherwise lack. Rudolf Otto insisted that the sense of the numinous must be excited or induced.[26] Liturgists appear to have paid little attention to how this can be done.

The tension between the "vertical" and the "horizontal" in liturgy is perhaps nowhere more evident than in the new custom by which Mass is celebrated with the priest facing the congregation. It is a rite which has unquestionably helped the people's understanding and sense of participation. At the same time it does tend to detract from the sense of an ordered solemn ceremony addressed to God. John Macquarrie has pointed out that some of the reformers who have most eagerly advocated this practice, such as the Anglican bishop John Robinson, are also proponents of a secularizing theology. Father Macquarrie has expressed a suspicion which has probably occurred to many people, even if liturgists did not intend it:

If a real God, transcending man and to whom one may offer worship, has become doubtful, then we must turn in upon ourselves and meditate on our own humanity and on what is going on in our midst.[27]

Josef Jungmann, noting that both the customs of facing toward the people and facing away from them are very ancient, added:

If Mass were only a service of instruction or a Communion celebration, the other position, facing the people, would be more natural. But it is different if the Mass is an immolation and homage to God.[28]

The communications theorist Marshall McLuhan has speculated that

. . . when the celebrant turns to the audience, he is putting them on as his corporate dignity or mask, just as when he turns to the altar, he is putting on the divine mask of supernatural power. A continuous confrontation of the audience by the celebrant reduces the occasion to the merely humanistic one. . . . "Putting on" only the congregation as his corporate mask of dignity, deprives the celebrant of any compelling power or charisma, and this fact is not lost on the young adults who, naturally, can think of no reason for seeking divine absolution nor for pursuing a merely banal vocation of a humanistic padre.[29]

The confusion of ultimate significances in the new liturgy badly needs to be clarified, in part because it is not evident to what extent the revised symbolism is doing what it was intended to do, and to what extent it has led to misconceptions. Some liturgists seem not to have understood the likely results of liturgical change, while others apparently intended all along to use liturgical change as a means of effecting revolution in belief. The great Anglican liturgist Gregory Dix noted that changes of rite always cause loss of meaning,[30] although they may also bring about the recovery of lost meaning. It is of the first importance now that the revised eucharistic symbolism not be allowed to effect a drastic secularization or protestantization of Catholic belief, either because these effects are not recognized and properly guarded against or because a handful of persons in strategic places deliberately set out to achieve them.

That such changes do have unanticipated and sometimes profound consequences has been admitted by one influential progressive liturgist. Referring to the practice of receiving communion in the hand, he said,

There is tremendous theological significance in the change. . . . I'm not sure, though, that it would be possible now to recoup the mystery of the old liturgy. . . . The communion has become a cheap commodity, cheaper than pizza, because you have to pay for pizza.[31]

NOTES

1. Tegels in *Worship*, XLII, 7 (August–September, 1968), p. 444.
2. *The Elizabethan Renaissance: the Life of the Society* (New York, 1971), p. 231.
3. *The England of Elizabeth: the Structure of Society* (London, 1951), p. 17.

4. *Natural Symbols*, p. 147.
5. *The Sacred Canopy* (Garden City, N.Y., 1967), p. 33.
6. "Religion as a Cultural System," *The Religious Situation: 1968*, ed. Donald R. Cutler (Boston, 1968), p. 642.
7. *The Mass of the Roman Rite*, trans. Francis A. Brunner, C.Ss.R, ed. Charles K. Riepe (New York, 1959), p. 200.
8. "Squalor on Sunday," *Worship*, XLIV, 5 (May, 1970), p. 293.
9. For example, Tegels in *Worship*, XLI, 1 (January, 1967), p. 55.
10. "Absurdity in Sacred Decoration," *Worship*, XXXIV, 5 (April, 1960), p. 248.
11. McManus, in *The Revival of the Liturgy*, (New York, 1963), p. 206.
12. Quoted in Yves M.-J. Congar, O.P., *Tradition and Traditions* (New York, 1967), p. 357.
13. Antoine Vergote, "Symbolic Gestures and Actions in the Liturgy," *Liturgy in Transition*, ed. H. Schmidt (*Concilium*, LXII [1971]), p. 43.
14. Gregory Baum, O.S.A., "Symbolism of Mass Has Been Clarified," *St. Louis Review*, October 22, 1971, p. 9; "Religion Is Powerful Social Force," *ibid.*, March 16, 1973, p. 7.
15. Reported in *St. Louis Review*, July 23, 1971, p. 9.
16. "Ritual Makers and Poverty of Proclamation," *Worship*, XLVI, 2 (January, 1972), pp. 69–75.
17. *Language in Worship* (New York, 1970), p. 87.
18. "The Political Identity of Catholics," *Commonweal*, February 16, 1973, p. 440.
19. *Language in Worship*, p. 42.
20. "Penitence, Relevance, and the Sense of the Sublime," *Towards a Living Liturgy*, ed. Donald Garfield (New York, 1969), p. 20.
21. *Natural Symbols*, pp. 19, 83, 154.
22. "Passages, Margins, and Poverty," *Worship*, XLVI, 7 (September, 1972), p. 392.
23. H. Marders, C.Ss.R., "Tradition and Renewal: the New Roman Anaphora," *Worship*, XLII, 10 (December, 1968), pp. 578–86.
24. *Language in Worship*, p. 37.
25. Tinsley, "Liturgy and Art," p. 76.
26. *The Idea of the Holy*, trans. John W. Harvey (New York, 1958), p. 60.
27. "Subjectivity and Objectivity in Theology and Worship," *Worship*, XLI, 3 (March, 1967), p. 158.
28. *The Mass of the Roman Rite*, pp. 181–82.
29. "Liturgy and Media," *The Critic*, XXXI, 4 (March–April, 1973), p. 70.
30. *The Shape of the Liturgy* (Westminster, England, 1952), p. xii.
31. Rev. Gerald Sigler. Quoted by William R. MacKaye in *The Washington Post*, November 16, 1973, p. D18.

CHAPTER 8

The Recovery of the Sacred

The decline of the sense of the sacred in worship during the past decade was not, as some reformers have argued, the inevitable effect of a secular age. If anything, advanced secular culture has shown itself more open to the sacred and the pseudo-sacred than at any time within memory. The spirit of pragmatic, technological rationality is in at least temporary disfavor, and the sacral worship of the Church was, paradoxically, more appealing and effective in the 1950s, when that spirit was more pervasive than it is now.

The decline of the sacred was, rather, something which was willed and planned: its demise was predicted by those who wished it to occur and who took steps to bring it about. To some extent also it occurred through inadvertence, by a process of liturgical change which gave little thought to long-term effects.

For many pepole this decline may be irreversible. Although nurtured within Catholicism, they have passed over into that kind of modern secularity which can see no point to religious ritual and which may even regard it with a certain loathing. For many others, however, it is still a genuine possibility. In large measure this is because the traditions of sacredness are still alive in the Church, among people for whom they were once quite strong. To a less extent there is a manifest hunger for such things among the supposedly secular younger generation. In any case the attempt to restore and revive sacral worship must occur before long, if it is to to be successful, because its most important foundation will be those traditions which are still alive but are becoming progressively weaker.

Until now no definition of the sacred has been offered, in part because it is almost that which cannot be defined, in part because it seems more useful to approach the phenomenon of liturgy empirically rather than with a priori categories. It may, however, be defined hesitatingly: the sacred in Catholicism is that awareness of God which is transmitted to believers through the media of religious symbols and rituals that are regarded as sharing in a divine character and are therefore worthy of themselves being considered sacred. This perception of God's reality is in tension between the sense of immanence and the sense of transcendence. God is perceived as present to the worshipers in a special way, but the symbols also point "beyond" or to an "other-world." There is simultaneously the attraction of love and the inhibition of awe. In the sacred symbols the whole life of the believer in the Church is perceived as being mystically incarnated and summed up.

A number of principles pertaining to this symbolic life have been formulated. To these several additional principles may be added:

The tendency to perceive religious faith primarily in interior, "spiritual" terms, with a corresponding indifference to its external expression, is an essentially Protestant attitude which is at odds with the spirit of Catholicism. Although Ca-

tholicism allows for private prayer and interior spiritual development, it insists that these be rooted in the public liturgy of the Church.

Thus for the most part Catholicism does not hold out the possibility of apprehending God directly, except in relatively rare cases, but rather, indirectly through symbols. Sacred ritual gives hints and intimations of the divine, but does not purport to offer a direct experience of God.

In sacred ritual the divine is deliberately hedged about by ancillary symbols which serve in part to "protect" it from too direct an attempt at apprehension.

Where these ancillary symbols are systematically removed, the divine center of the ritual tends to elude participants.

Therefore, in sacred ritual small things can be of great importance and an attitude of compulsive puritanism tends to the destruction of the meaning of the entire ritual.

A sense of the sacred depends in part on a sense of awe or reverence which is capable of being violated. Hence a deliberate iconoclasm or a deliberate casualness in liturgy, insofar as these come to be accepted, signal the death of the sacred.

It is easier and less potentially destructive to add new levels of symbolism to the rite than to eliminate older ones.

The sense of the sacred depends in part on the liturgy's being conducted in an appropriately dramatic manner, which implies a special architecture, special vestments, and recognizably religious symbolism.

This sense adheres at least as much in the use of physical objects—the sacred species of Communion, holy water, candles, rosary beads, etc.—as in words or thoughts.

Sacred ritual is a tight network of meanings in which nothing is entirely meaningless and the various elements are related to each other in ways not always immediately perceptible. Thus alterations in this network can have the effect

*of unraveling the whole, even if apparently trivial changes
are made.*

*Sacred liturgy is heavily based on certain temporal
rhythms which become part of the psychic makeup of the
believer, thus helping to internalize beliefs and keep them
alive outside the times of formal worship. These cycles are
primarily those of the Church year but also, for example, the
distinction between Sunday and weekdays or, formerly, the
special significance of Friday for Roman Catholics. The drastic abrogation of these cycles tends to weaken drastically
the meaning which underlies them.*

That the decline of the sacred was primarily willed and
planned and did not simply occur is evident from the remarks of numerous liturgists in the postconciliar period (see
Chapter 1). Since this willed desacralization went contrary
to the desires of many people in the Church, and has been
for many the most profoundly disturbing aspect of renewal,
it is not irreversible. Unlike certain other facets of discarded
tradition, it could be restored not by papal or episcopal fiat
but by the joyful cooperation of many lay people. The details of this restoration will inevitably require thought and
occasion some disagreement. Its need, however, seems undeniable if the Catholic Church is to preserve its unique
traditions of spirituality and even its primary reason for existing. For as Louis Bouyer had said even before liturgical
reform began:

The Incarnation therefore does not efface or render useless or
outmoded the primitive notion of the sacred—of a domain "set
apart," as the word indicates, in the life of man to belong wholly
to God and God alone. How could it do this without abolishing
even man's sense of God as of a being distinct from man, independent of him, but sovereign alike over him and all things? [1]

. . . there is all the more reason that our adoptions of the liturgy should not attempt to rationalize it, to empty it not only of its mystery but also of all its expressions that are not strictly rational. They should, on the contrary, seize again upon the chords in the heart of man which respond to these eternal expressions in order to restore to them their maximum efficacy. At the same time, we must do everything in our power to revive man's atrophied faculties. It will be necessary to restore to the essential liturgical symbols their living richness which has been sadly weakened by our own rationalism. But it will be equally necessary to strive to bring back to our contemporaries a religious culture that will be human to the extent that it is also biblical. . . .[2]

Based on the principles formulated above, some suggestions can now be made as to how a sense of the sacred might be rekindled:

• Liturgy should assume that the worshiper is *Homo religiosus*. Despite the claims of those who invoke the name of Bonhoeffer, man's religious sense has not dried up, nor is it likely to. In the Catholic Church especially there is much evidence of hunger for a truly sacral worship which is not being filled and which is driving Catholics to seek for religious experience in movements like Pentecostalism. To the degree that liturgy tries to appeal to "secular man" in his own terms it is self-defeating and it squanders the liturgical riches of the Church.

• Although contemporary references are naturally appropriate in homilies and petitions, they should for the most part be omitted from the eucharistic rite itself. If introduced sparingly they tend to jar in the context of the generally uncontemporary style of the service. If they dominate the rite, its fundamental meaning is undermined. In either case they tend to subvert the rite to immediate practical ends it was not meant to serve, and they produce confusion and tension in the symbolism. (For example, a newly ordained priest celebrates in a chasuble decorated with the eagle of the

United Farm Workers.[3] However just the cause, such immediacy tends to distract from the eternal dimension which is supposed to be at the heart of the ritual. An American flag would be equally inappropriate, even if celebrant and congregation were intensely patriotic. It is in fact unfortunate that American flags are so commonly found in church sanctuaries, although they and farm workers' emblems might have a place somewhere else in the church.)

• Noneucharistic forms of spontaneous devotion should be encouraged, whether through the revival of older cults or the development of new forms like prayer groups.

• As a corollary to this, there should be renewed emphasis on the Eucharist as a great, public, objective act which transcends, although it also subsumes, the private concerns of particular peoples and individuals. Elements of casualness and spontaneity are for the most part inappropriate in this kind of rite. Above all, worshipers should not be taught to expect a necessary correspondence between their immediate subjective feelings and the words and themes of the rite. A habitual acceptance of the major thrust of the liturgy is, rather, what is required, and it is self-defeating to attempt to "reform" liturgy for the sake of those who are unsympathetic to its basic purpose and character.

• There is need for general liturgical uniformity and officially prescribed rites, although a degree of variety has always existed and can exist provided it is not extreme. The notion of a continually changing liturgy subject to local experimental variations is subversive of public liturgy and hence subversive of the public existence of the Church. Liturgical experimentation cannot in the nature of things be successfully inhibited, but it is important that the Church distinguish clearly and forcefully between what is official liturgy and what is not.

• Steps should be taken to reestablish as much as possible a sense of continuity with the Church's historical past which, because of the doctrine of the Communion of Saints, can never be merely a dead past. This includes the restoration of discarded symbols, the reintroduction of the saints into the Canon of the Mass (preferably not just the obscure early ones of the old liturgy), and a renewed attention to the calendar of the saints in homilies and prayers. The bias of liturgical thought needs to shift from desiring to be as innovative as possible while maintaining tenuous contact with tradition to conserving as many traditions as still have validity.

• In this connection Catholic liturgy should be accepted as a historical development through time, periodically in need of revision and purification. The ideal of returning to the "pure" liturgy of the early Church, which in any case is unattainable, should be discarded.

• A liturgy which is truly biblical in spirit will generally prove more compatible with the traditional liturgy of the Church, albeit reformed, than with extreme purifications which tend to adopt the spirit of contemporary secular culture.

• Participation in liturgy should be regarded as primarily the joining in a timeless and eternal rite, made possible through symbols. Jarring incongruities should be avoided, such as the suggestion that in the penitential rite worshipers ask pardon for failing to say, "Come in. You're welcome. Forget it," for "the days we 'clam up.' "[4] An entire Mass in contemporary speech is a barely conceivable possibility; snippets of contemporaneity are merely distracting.

• The sense of the liturgy as a timeless ritual act depends on an attitude of deliberate reverence, care, and solemnity on the part of the celebrant, joined in by the congregation. Gestures should be stylized and deliberate, vestments and images chosen carefully, words proclaimed and not rendered conversationally.

• In Catholicism the sermon or homily has always served

as a moratorium in solemn liturgies, partly as a time of didactic instruction different in spirit from most of the liturgy itself, partly as a relaxation from the formal atmosphere of the ritual. The personal element, the conversational tone, the particular needs of the worshiping community, and humor have their place here and not elsewhere in the Mass.

• The liturgy should be perceived as reflecting and symbolizing a basic Christian sense of order and certitude which underlies all human anxieties and confusions. Real Catholic liturgy is therefore impossible apart from a believing acceptance of this order and this certitude. Liturgies which reflect the confusions of the participants are self-destructive.

• Where a strong sense of community exists among worshipers, this will be a significant part of the liturgical celebration. However, it is neither possible nor desirable to develop this sense where it does not already exist, since for Catholics the worshiping community is much broader than simply a particular congregation. The greeting of peace is best seen as a ritual gesture, for example, not as a spontaneous act.

• Sacred symbols should not be used to convey meanings different from their traditional meanings. Mircea Eliade has said that while the meaning of archaic symbols can be extended or deepened, they cannot be altered or destroyed.[5] The attempt to alter them tends to produce psychic disorientation and the disintegration of the rite.

• Vital liturgy inevitably grows out of the most profound beliefs of the worshipers. Hence it should be recognized that true worship cannot at present be ecumenical in any broad sense but must be the expression of special religious identities. Where ecumenical liturgy does occur this must represent the dscovery of profound agreements not previously recognized. Where it rests merely on the spirit of good will it tends to drain the sacred symbols of their power.

• The traditions of the Church must be conceded genuine

authority in liturgy as in other matters. Hence departures from these traditions should be sparing and carefully considered. The sense of the sacred depends heavily on the sense of tradition lying behind it.

• Genuine Catholic liturgy is not possible without an acceptance of the legitimacy and authority of the Church. The tendency simply to use Catholic ritual for private purposes is corrupting of that liturgy.

• The validity and effectiveness of the ritual depends heavily on its being seen as public and official. Hence the importance of compulsory Sunday Mass attendance or, when it was in effect, the compulsory Friday abstinence. Insofar, as rites are seen as primarily a matter of personal preference, they lose much of their significance.

• The Church requires official public rites for its coherence and unity. Thus, on the whole, it is better to celebrate Mass in public buildings like churches than in private places, although the latter practice has a valid but limited use. It is better on the whole to have heterogeneous congregations participating in uniform liturgies.

• The puritan mentality should be recognized as, on the whole, a destructive feature of contemporary liturgical life. Every effort should be made to restore a worship which is rich, complex, and even occasionally ornate. The use of incense, bells, candles, and traditional gestures should be revived where it has lapsed. Signs of the cross, genuflections, and breast-beatings should be reinstated while they still have meaning for many worshipers.

• Habits of prayer and devotion are fostered and kept alive not only through verbal or mental prayer but also through what might be called "muscular memories"—familiar ritual gestures which summon up for the actor a range of implicit beliefs. Genuflecting before a tabernacle or making the sign of the cross with holy water on entering a church are examples of this. So also is the fingering of rosary beads.

Such actions can have religious meaning even without conscious reflection, because they operate on a deeper level of the mind.

• Systematic instruction is necessary in the full meaning of the Mass, particularly its sacrificial nature and its character as a timeless mystical action. By default much of this meaning has been lost since the Second Vatican Council, and in some cases has been deliberately undermined. Without some understanding of this theology, the deepest significance of the rite is missed and its importance greatly reduced, since the idea of the Mass as community meal is neither rich enough nor profound enough to sustain the weight of this most sacred of Catholic acts.

• To present ritual acts, for example the sacraments, primarily as symbols intended to convey a message is to impoverish them. Religious rituals are also manifestations of divine power in the world, and their deepest significance lies in the worshipers' sense of this power. This should be emphasized even at the risk that some people will regard the rites as magical.

• The power of sacred symbols is partly proportionate to their being recognizably strange within the context of everyday life, as having no evident commonsense meaning. (The crucifix, representing the great "scandal" of Christianity, is perhaps the most powerful of these, or the transformation of bread and wine into Christ's body and blood.) When the priest's prostration on Good Friday is dismissed as "melodramatic and altogether foreign to our culture," [6] for example, the main point of sacred symbolism has been lost and the thrust of liturgical reform directed in a way that is bound to weaken the symbolism, not make it more meaningful.

• Although religious ritual needs to be intelligible to worshipers in at least its fundamental meanings and its major contours, too great a concern with the intelligibility of the rites tends to be counter-productive. As Louis Bouyer has pointed out:

. . . , as soon as one considers religious symbolism, and especially ritualistic symbolism, as an action conceived *post-factum* to illustrate ideas that were first developed in the abstract, this symbolism will never more be understood.[7]

The "fallacy of explicitness" has been responsible for much of the liturgical impoverishment of the past decade, since some liturgists (and some worshipers) appeared to assume that once the symbols had been "explained" there was no longer any need for them. The goal of some liturgical reform appeared to be that of translating as many symbols as possible into words, with the eventual elimination of symbols altogether.

• Certain aspects of ritual have validity less in terms of specific, explicable meanings than in serving to create and sustain the proper atmosphere of sacredness. The blessing with holy water upon entering a church, incense and candles, the numerous genuflections and signs of the cross are all symbols which can be "explained" in one or more ways, but which serve primarily this more general purpose. There is a danger here that symbols may become mere "signs," no longer pointing beyond themselves but seen as merely referring to the rite itself.[9] However, as Claude Lévi-Strauss has noted:

A native thinker makes the penetrating comment that "All sacred things must be in their place." . . . It could even be said that being in their place is what makes them sacred for if they were taken out of their place, even in thought, the entire order of the universe would be destroyed. Sacred objects therefore contribute to the maintenance of order in the universe by occupying the places allocated to them.[9]

- The reformed liturgy is presently too bare and direct, which has led to the decline of a sense of the sacred and of its character as a mystery. There needs to be a restoration of subordinate ritual acts which serve in a sense to hedge the central mystery about, even if these seem from one point of view arbitrary.
- The alteration of traditional subordinate rituals has resulted in consequences which for the most part were not foreseen. The central act of the Eucharist was, for example, formerly "protected" by a whole series of rites intended to impress on the worshiper a sense of the holiness of the Mass itself—the blessing with holy water at the door of the church, the genuflection before entering the pew, silence before Mass, kneeling during Mass, the Communion rail separating the sanctuary from the body of the church, the eucharistic vessels handled only by the priest, Communion given only from his hands, the paten held to catch crumbs from the Host, etc. The Eucharist could in theory be celebrated without any of these surrounding rites, as liturgists have often pointed out. However, having been long established and deeply impressed on worshipers' minds, it was impossible that these rites could be altered or eliminated without conveying the impression (perhaps unconscious) that the central meaning of the Eucharist was being changed. A Dominican theologian has speculated, for example, that the changes in the Roman missal were intended to "correct" traditional Catholic belief about the Real Presence,[10] and numerous Catholics have reached a similar conclusion, although this was certainly not the intention of the Second Vatican Council. The proposal to authorize laymen to take Communion in their hands cannot help but reinforce this same impression among Roman Catholics, where the contrary practice has been deeply ingrained, even though it probably causes no difficulty among Anglo-Catholics be-

cause it has been so long established among them. A ritual which is theoretically unobjectionable may take on an unwanted significance when it involves the dramatic alteration of existing customs. For example, the removal of the tabernacle from the high altar in many churches, although usually done with good intentions, cannot help but appear symbolically as the "dethroning" of the sacrament. It has helped diminish eucharistic piety.

• There is greater need than ever to insist on the official and traditional meaning of liturgical symbols, since both the Church's unity of belief and the meaning of the central liturgical rites are in danger of fragmenting. For example, the color of vestments does not simply represent the Church's indulging in "precise ordering of lives," and the proposal that "Any color, any day should be acceptable, including plaids, dashikis, and ponchos if they reflect the community" [11] is merely an admission that liturgy has become a kind of Happening and does not symbolize some deep religious order. Even when worshipers do not know the explicit symbolism of a particular color (most of the time it is fairly obvious), they do recognize that the variation of colors represents the structure of a sacred year with its seasons and feasts. The alternative is to lose touch with this structure and to reduce the liturgical celebration to a merely private one.

• The rekindling of a vivid faith requires at the present time a recovery of a sense of the importance of what Blaise Pascal called "custom" in religion—that which leads from the external to the internal, which governs the body, which in turn "persuades the mind without its thinking about the matter." As Pascal also said, "It is superstition to put one's hopes in formalities; but it is pride to be unwilling to submit to them." [12] A. R. Radcliffe-Brown pointed out that belief can be the fruit of ritual participation, rather than the other way around,[13] and the crisis of belief in the Catholic Church is clearly related to the crisis of liturgy, one reinforcing the other. To an astonishing degree Catholics appear no longer to pray privately or in meetings of their organizations, clerical or lay, although it is a virtual certainty that people who say no private prayers will be unable to pray in the liturgy either. This decline of prayer is partly due to an unrealistic and un-Catholic tendency to regard prayer as essentially an interior, subjective experience and the corresponding acceptance of the puritan notion that spontaneous prayer is superior to set prayer. The prayer life of Catholics could begin to revitalize itself if they would once again undertake the simple disciplines formerly associated with it—kneeling, making the sign of the cross, reciting familiar prayers, dropping into church for private devotions, etc. For many people over the centuries such a regimen has led to a steadily deepening prayer life. In the words of the great lay theologian Baron Friedrich von Hügel:

As a matter of fact, a wholesome sense of the infinite arises and is renewed, within us, not only by recollection but also by contact with the contingent, with matter, time, and space. It is not only that we have a body and (partly physical) fellow-creatures. . . . but that *the sense of the infinite and of the finite spring up together and condition each other.* Hence we shall never attain a thoroughly wholesome, deeply spiritual religion, unless we take care to give it, and to keep for it, a body.

It is no doubt certain that at the time of such attention to particular, institutional acts—the kneeling for, and the recitation of, formal vocal prayers, the attending of church services, even the reception of Holy Communion—we often feel as though contracted, as though these things were dry and petty; and as though God, Spirit and Infinite, must be right outside all such temptations and materialities.

Yet life shows us everywhere how necessary, for our fuller expansion and true deepening, are such seemingly narrowing, humblingly obscure contacts with the visible—such contractions of our attention and feeling to *things,* to matter, to the little Here and Now. . . . *religion requires some apparently unnecessary, emotionally more or less irksome contractions and attentions to visible and audibly institutional and social acts and rites.* Without *some* such, we cannot fully capture and maintain a deep wholesome recollection and spirituality.[14]

• Liturgists need to respect much more than in the past the spirit and forms of popular piety in the Church, to accommodate these as much as possible, and to integrate them with official worship. Few things have been more destructive both of prayer and of the peace of the Church than the war waged on popular piety by some of the clergy.

• A certain theological and liturgical diversity is unavoidable in the present age of the Church, although it should not be multiplied deliberately and unnecessarily. However, it is important that Church authorities officially disavow that which appears simply to use Catholic liturgy as a starting point for celebrations of a different character. Tolerance for broad liturgical experimentation inevitably robs the official liturgy of much of its significance and produces an atmosphere of confusion and incoherence.

• The Latin liturgy must regain a place in the living worship of the Church, to which all Catholics have regular access. Pope Paul VI has suggested that it might be retained in the *Gloria, Credo, Sanctus,* and *Agnus Dei.*[15] An alternative might be for every reasonably large parish to provide one Latin Mass each Sunday at a convenient time. It would be particularly effective if this were a High Mass sung by congregation and choir together. Parishioners might then be encouraged to familiarize themselves with both Latin and vernacular worship on a regular basis and not identify themselves exclusively with either.

• The Roman Catholic Church in America badly needs a new English text for the Mass, prepared with greater regard for linguistic dignity and power. Pointlessly truncated prayers like the *Confiteor* should be restored to their full versions.

• There is also, however, a great need in America for liturgical stability, which is in obvious conflict with the previous need. The preparation of a new translation would in any case take some years. The need for liturgical stability ought also to give pause to those traditionalists who would like simply to return to the Mass of Pius V and abolish the changes of the past decade. Such a move would precipitate crises and disorientations comparable to those previously caused by the move to the vernacular.

• Historically, Catholic churches have often been used for profane purposes as well as sacred ones. Paradoxically, however, this was more easily tolerable in ages when people believed in the sacred implicitly and deeply, when religion permeated every aspect of culture and society. At the present time a sharp symbolic separation of sacred and profane is necessary if the sacred is not simply to be absorbed into an amorphous atmosphere of humanistic good feeling. Thus the symbolism of the church building as a place set apart is of great importance, and churches should be used for functions other than worship only sparingly. This corresponds to the sense which many modern Catholics have that the spaces where they can pray and carry on their worship are hard won amid pervasive secularity and religious indifference, and must be protected.

• Rituals can be made more symbolically meaningful by the introduction of certain new elements which are nonetheless in harmony with the basic beliefs and traditions of the Church. These might include, for example, Communion under both kinds by the laity and Baptism by immersion. The use of a more substantial Communion bread than wafers is in the same spirit, although ordinary table bread seems inappropriate. The Church can now afford to err on the side of too much drama and symbolism in its rites, because of the excessive pruning of the past decade.

• Strong efforts should be made to reemphasize the cycles of the sacred calendar and particularly to rescue many formerly familiar saints who are now in danger of falling into obscurity. The Friday abstinence, which was a burden to practically no one and which was abolished for no apparent good reason, should be restored while it is still meaningful to many people. It was one of the most important symbols of folk Catholicism. The Lenten fast, which is now confused in most people's minds, should be clarified and reemphasized.

• Although a surfeit of technical ecclesiastical and liturgical language has a deadening effect on religious life, the existence of the sacred implies a special sacral language whose terms are largely unintelligible to outsiders. From one point of view this appears as sheer obscurantism. However, the linguist Basil Bernstein has distinguished the "restricted code" of speech from the "elaborated code." The latter is a mode of address by which explicit meanings are communicated verbally by one individual to another, and the former is language used to address a fellow member of the same social group in terms of shared assumptions. The elaborated code seeks to impart information; the restricted code seeks to reaffirm identities. Users of each code often find it impossible to imagine conditions under which use of the other would be possible. There is to some extent a class bias involved, in that educated children of the middle class are more likely to develop the elaborated code and children of the lower classes to retain the restricted code.[16] The sudden disappearance of so much liturgical and devotional language in the past decade—words like "novena," "indulgence," "fast day," even "Mass"—has had the effect of weakening the sense of community in the Church and the special significance of its rites.

• A sense of the sacred requires correspondingly a sense

of the possibility of sacrilege, a concept which strangely has
been kept alive in recent years not so much by Catholics as
by infidels—there have been reports of tabernacles being
robbed more frequently and of black Masses being celebrated. Such incidents are, from one standpoint, merely fad-
dish and melodramatic. However, in the act of sacrilege
what is important is not so much what happens to the sacred
objects as how believers regard such actions. It is true that
God cannot be harmed by sacrilege. It is equally true that
Catholics who refuse to be moved by such acts testify to
their own diminished faith in the reality of the sacred. If
religious belief is worthy of certain external manifestations,
these manifestations are also worthy of being cherished and
protected.

• The use of the Mass by Leonard Bernstein and others
as a "symbol of ultimacy" testifies to its continued power in
modern culture. For that very reason Catholics should resist
and dissociate themselves from all such efforts to appropriate its power for essentially secular purposes. In the usual
practice of fashionable modernism, it will be used so long as
it appears to have vitality, then will be discarded when the
vitality has been siphoned off.

• A related danger is a revived interest in "high," solemn
liturgy for reasons which are primarily esthetic and are di-
vorced from the traditional beliefs that alone make such liturgy meaningful. Such a revival is a strong probability in the
near future, in reaction to the often shallow contemporaneity
of the past decade. Such estheticism also renders the ritual
ultimately meaningless; it is merely another form of liturgy
as Happening.

The crisis of worship currently affecting the Church is
perhaps the most serious of its many crises, since the ultimate life and unity of the Church is expressed first of all in
the liturgy, which comprises the Church's great and central
acts. Although men of good will might prefer that it be

otherwise, this crisis will not be successfully weathered without making hard choices and without much care and thought. A general condition of liturgical drift, if it continues, will end by rendering much of the Church's worship ineffective and incomprehensible even to believers. To an unfortunate extent the authentic spirit of the Liturgical Movement was dissipated in the frenzied atmosphere which followed the Second Vatican Council. It needs now to be recovered if the Council's hope is to be realized that through the liturgy "the human is directed and subordinated to the divine, the visible likewise to the invisible, action to contemplation, and this present world to that city yet to come, which we seek." [17]

NOTES

1. "Two Temptations," *Worship*, XXXVII, 1 (December, 1962), p. 18.
2. *Rite and Man* (South Bend, 1963), p. 220.
3. See picture in *Maryknoll*, October, 1973, p. 39.
4. *Celebration*, July, 1973.
5. *The Sacred and the Profane*, trans. Willard R. Trask (New York, 1959), p. 137.
6. Avery, "Holy Week Reexamined," *Worship*, XLI, 3 (March, 1967), p. 177.
7. *Rite and Man*, p. 63.
8. Fernandez, "Symbolic Consensus," *American Anthropologist*, LXVII, 4 (August, 1965), pp. 917–18.
9. *The Savage Mind* (Chicago, 1966), p. 10.
10. Brian Rice McCarthy, O.P., in *Commonweal*, November 17, 1972, p. 167.
11. Nolan, in *The National Catholic Reporter*, March 16, 1973, p. 9, and February 25, 1972, p. 6.
12. *Pensées* (with *The Provincial Letters*), (Modern Library edn., 1941), pp. 88–89.
13. *Structure and Function in Primitive Society* (Glencoe, Ill., 1952), p. 155.

14. Quoted in Joseph P. Whelan, S.J., *The Spirituality of Friedrich von Hügel* (New York, 1971), pp. 230–31. Italics in original.

15. Quoted in *St. Louis Review,* August 31, 1973, p. 5.

16. "Elaborated and Restricted Codes: Their Social Origins and Some Consequences," in *Communication and Culture,* ed. Alfred G. Smith (New York, 1966), pp. 437–40.

17. *The Documents of Vatican II,* ed. Abbott (New York, 1966), p. 138.